my **revisi⏻n** notes

Edexcel AS/A-level

POLITICS

US POLITICS

Anthony J Bennett

Series Editor: Eric Magee

HODDER
EDUCATION
AN HACHETTE UK COMPANY

Orders: please contact Bookpoint Ltd, 130 Park Drive, Milton Park, Abingdon, Oxon OX14 4SE. Telephone: (44) 01235 827827. Fax: (44) 01235 400401. Email education@bookpoint.co.uk Lines are open from 9 a.m. to 5 p.m., Monday to Saturday, with a 24-hour message answering service. You can also order through our website: www.hoddereducation.co.uk

ISBN: 978 1 4718 8963 9

© Anthony J Bennett 2018

First published in 2018 by
Hodder Education,
An Hachette UK Company
Carmelite House
50 Victoria Embankment
London EC4Y 0DZ

www.hoddereducation.co.uk

Impression number   10 9 8 7 6 5 4 3 2

Year   2022 2021 2020 2019

Cover photo: Marina Riley/Alamy
Typeset by Integra Software Services Pvt. Ltd., Pondicherry, India
Printed in Spain

A catalogue record for this title is available from the British Library.

Get the most from this book

Everyone has to decide his or her own revision strategy, but it is essential to review your work, learn it and test your understanding. These Revision Notes will help you to do that in a planned way, topic by topic. Use this book as the cornerstone of your revision and don't hesitate to write in it — personalise your notes and check your progress by ticking off each section as you revise.

Tick to track your progress

Use the revision planner on pages 4 and 5 to plan your revision, topic by topic. Tick each box when you have:

● revised and understood a topic
● tested yourself
● practised the exam questions and gone online to check your answers and complete the quick quizzes

You can also keep track of your revision by ticking off each topic heading in the book. You may find it helpful to add your own notes as you work through each topic.

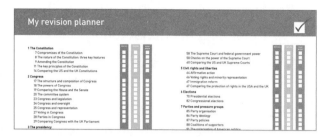

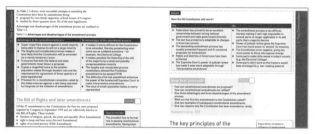

Features to help you succeed

Exam tips

Expert tips are given throughout the book to help you polish your exam technique in order to maximise your chances in the exam.

Typical mistakes

The author identifies the typical mistakes candidates make and explains how you can avoid them.

Now test yourself

These short, knowledge-based questions provide the first step in testing your learning. Answers are at the back of the book.

Definitions and key words

Clear, concise definitions of essential key terms are provided where they first appear.

Key words from the specification are highlighted in bold throughout the book.

Debates

Debates are highlighted to help you assess arguments and use evidence appropriately.

Summaries

The summaries provide a quick-check bullet list for each topic.

Exam practice

Practice exam questions are provided for each topic. Use them to consolidate your revision and practise your exam skills.

Online

Go online to check your answers to the exam questions and try out the extra quick quizzes at **www.hoddereducation.co.uk/myrevisionnotesdownloads**

My revision planner

REVISED   TESTED   EXAM READY

Now test yourself answers

Exam practice answers and quick quizzes at
www.hoddereducation.co.uk/myrevisionnotesdownloads

Countdown to my exams

6–8 weeks to go

- Start by looking at the specification — make sure you know exactly what material you need to revise and the style of the examination. Use the revision planner on pages 4 and 5 to familiarise yourself with the topics.
- Organise your notes, making sure you have covered everything on the specification. The revision planner will help you to group your notes into topics.
- Work out a realistic revision plan that will allow you time for relaxation. Set aside days and times for all the subjects that you need to study, and stick to your timetable.
- Set yourself sensible targets. Break your revision down into focused sessions of around 40 minutes, divided by breaks. These Revision Notes organise the basic facts into short, memorable sections to make revising easier.

REVISED

2–6 weeks to go

- Read through the relevant sections of this book and refer to the exam tips, exam summaries, typical mistakes and key terms. Tick off the topics as you feel confident about them. Highlight those topics you find difficult and look at them again in detail.
- Test your understanding of each topic by working through the 'Now test yourself' questions in the book. Look up the answers at the back of the book.
- Make a note of any problem areas as you revise, and ask your teacher to go over these in class.
- Look at past papers. They are one of the best ways to revise and practise your exam skills. Write or prepare planned answers to the exam practice questions provided in this book. Check your answers online and try out the extra quick quizzes at **www.hoddereducation. co.uk/myrevisionnotesdownloads**
- Use the revision activities to try out different revision methods. For example, you can make notes using mind maps, spider diagrams or flash cards.
- Track your progress using the revision planner and give yourself a reward when you have achieved your target.

REVISED

One week to go

- Try to fit in at least one more timed practice of an entire past paper and seek feedback from your teacher, comparing your work closely with the mark scheme.
- Check the revision planner to make sure you haven't missed out any topics. Brush up on any areas of difficulty by talking them over with a friend or getting help from your teacher.
- Attend any revision classes put on by your teacher. Remember, he or she is an expert at preparing people for examinations.

REVISED

The day before the examination

- Flick through these Revision Notes for useful reminders, for example the exam tips, exam summaries, typical mistakes and key terms.
- Check the time and place of your examination.
- Make sure you have everything you need — extra pens and pencils, tissues, a watch, bottled water, sweets.
- Allow some time to relax and have an early night to ensure you are fresh and alert for the examinations.

REVISED

My exams

Component 1

Date:..

Time:..

Location: ....

Component 2

Date:..

Time:..

Location: ....

Component 3

Date:..

Time:..

Location: ....

1 The Constitution

Compromises of the Constitution

The form of government

REVISED

Under British control, the colonies had been ruled under a unitary form of government – one in which political power rests with one central/national government (of Great Britain in this case).

From 1781, they had been ruled under a confederal form of government – one in which virtually all political power rests with the individual states and little with the central/national government.

The compromise was to devise a new form of government – a federal form of government, one in which some political power rests with the national (known as the federal) government, but other, equally important, powers rest with the state governments.

> **Exam tip**
>
> Notice 'equally important' – it's crucial to include that phrase so as not to give the impression that the state governments' powers are trivial.

Representation of the states

- Large-population states wanted representation in Congress to be proportional to population: the bigger the population of a state, the more representatives it would have in Congress.
- Small-population states wanted equal representation.
- The compromise was to have Congress made up of two houses – the House of Representatives and the Senate.
- In the House of Representatives, there would be representation proportional to population.
- In the Senate, there would be equal representation for all states, regardless of population.

> **Typical mistake**
>
> Don't use the phrase 'proportional representation' – it isn't!

Choosing the president

There were many different suggestions about how to choose the president.
- Some thought the president should be appointed.
- Others thought the president should be directly elected by the people.
- The compromise was to have the president indirectly elected by an Electoral College (see Chapter 6).

> **Exam tip**
>
> To save yourself time in the exam, use the term 'House' (with a capital H) to refer to the House of Representatives.

> **Now test yourself**
>
> TESTED
>
> 1 What was wrong with the Articles of Confederation?
> 2 Give three examples of compromises in the Constitution.
>
> Answers on p. 107

The nature of the Constitution: three key features

The Constitution has three key features:

1 It is codified.
2 Some of it is specific but some of it is vague.
3 Its provisions are entrenched.

A codified Constitution

● 'Codified' is not a word we use in everyday language, but you will be familiar with the idea of a code in this sense. If you learn to drive, you will need to study the Highway Code – the collected and authoritative rules for all road users. Many organisations will have a 'code of conduct'. Your school or college will probably call them 'rules'.

● Some constitutions, like that for the UK, are uncodified – they are not collected together in one document – while others, such as that of the USA, are codified. There is one document called the Constitution.

● But it's worth remembering that these two terms are not exclusive to one another, and they are not the same as 'written' and 'unwritten' constitutions. **Codified constitutions** may not include all constitutional provisions. Written constitutions may have some elements that are unwritten.

> **Codified constitution:** A Constitution that consists of a full and authoritative set of rules written down in a single document.

The new constitution was made up of seven Articles, the first three of which explained how the three branches of the federal (national) government would work and what powers they would have (see Table 1.1).

Table 1.1 Summary of Articles I, II and III of the Constitution

Article I	Established Congress as the national legislature (law-making body), defined its membership, method of election and powers
Article II	Established the president as chief executive, defined method of election and powers
Article III	Established the United States Supreme Court and set out membership, method of appointment and powers

Table 1.1 also shows that these first three Articles set out the powers of Congress, the president and the Supreme Court. That leads us to the second of the Constitution's three key features – that some of it is specific and some of it is vague.

A blend of specificity and vagueness

Some of the powers the Constitution gives, especially to Congress, are very specific:

● the power 'to collect taxes' (Article I)
● the power 'to coin money' (Article I).

But others are quite vague:

● the power of Congress 'to provide for the common defence and general welfare of the United States' (Article I)
● the power of Congress 'to make all laws which shall be necessary and proper for carrying into execution the foregoing powers' (Article I).

There is also the issue of whether certain powers belong only to the federal government, only to the state governments, or to both the federal and state governments. Table 1.2 explains these different types of powers.

Table 1.2 Summary of different types of powers of the Constitution

Enumerated (or delegated) powers	Powers delegated to the federal government – generally those enumerated in the first three Articles of the Constitution
Implied powers	Powers possessed by the federal government by inference from those powers delegated to it in the Constitution
Reserved powers	Powers not delegated to the federal government, or prohibited to them by the Constitution, are reserved to the states or to the people
Concurrent powers	Powers possessed by both the federal and state governments

Entrenched provisions

Entrenchment is written into the Constitution by the complicated and demanding process for amending it.

> **Entrenchment**: The application of extra legal safeguards to a constitutional provision to make it more difficult to amend or abolish it.

Now test yourself

TESTED

3 What are the three key features of the Constitution?
4 What is a codified constitution?
5 What do the first three articles of the Constitution deal with?
6 Give an example of the vagueness of the Constitution.
7 What is the difference between enumerated powers and implied powers?
8 What is the difference between reserved powers and concurrent powers?
9 What does 'entrenchment' mean?

Answers on p. 107

Amending the Constitution

The various methods for amending the Constitution are set out in Table 1.3.

Table 1.3 The process for amending the Constitution

	Proposed by	Ratified by	How often used?
1	Two-thirds of the House and the Senate	Three-quarters of the state legislatures (38)	26 times
2	Two-thirds of the House and the Senate	Ratifying conventions in three-quarters of the states	Once (Twenty-first Amendment)
3	Legislatures in two-thirds of the states calling for a national constitutional convention	Three-quarters of the state legislatures	Never
4	Legislatures in two-thirds of the states calling for a national constitutional convention	Ratifying conventions in three-quarters of the states	Never

As Table 1.3 shows, most successful attempts at amending the Constitution have been by amendments being:
- proposed by two-thirds majorities of both houses of Congress
- ratified by three-quarters (now 38) of the state legislatures.

Advantages and disadvantages of the amendment process are outlined in Table 1.4.

Table 1.4 Advantages and disadvantages of the amendment process

Advantages of the amendment process	Disadvantages of the amendment process
• Super-majorities ensure against a small majority being able to impose its will on a large minority • The lengthy and complicated process makes it less likely that the Constitution will be amended on a merely temporary issue • It ensures that both the federal and state governments must favour a proposal • It gives a magnified voice to the smaller-population states (through Senate's role and the requirement for agreement of three-quarters of state legislatures) • Provision for a constitutional convention called by the states ensures against a veto being operated by Congress on the initiation of amendments	• It makes it overly difficult for the Constitution to be amended, thereby perpetuating what some see as outdated provisions – for example, the Electoral College • It makes possible the thwarting of the will of the majority by a small and possibly unrepresentative minority • The lengthy and complicated process nonetheless allowed the Prohibition amendment to be passed (1918) • The difficulty of formal amendment enhances the power of the (unelected) Supreme Court to make interpretative amendments • The voice of small-population states is overly represented

The Bill of Rights and later amendments

REVISED

Of the 27 amendments to the Constitution, the first ten were proposed together by Congress in September 1789 and are collectively known as the Bill of Rights. These include:
- freedom of religion, speech, the press and assembly (First Amendment)
- right to keep and bear arms (Second Amendment)
- rights of accused persons (Fifth Amendment)
- cruel and unusual punishments prohibited (Eighth Amendment)
- undelegated powers reserved to the states or to the people (Tenth Amendment).

Amendments added later include:
- slavery prohibited (Thirteenth Amendment, 1865)
- federal government granted power to impose income tax (Sixteenth Amendment, 1913)
- direct election of the Senate (Seventeenth Amendment, 1913)
- two-term limit for the president (Twenty-second Amendment, 1951)
- presidential succession and disability procedures (Twenty-fifth Amendment, 1967)
- voting age lowered to 18 (Twenty-sixth Amendment, 1971).

There have been only 27 successful attempts to amend the Constitution and only 15 since 1805. That is pretty infrequent. So why has the Constitution been so rarely amended? Reasons include:
- the Founding Fathers created a deliberately difficult process
- the Constitution is, in parts, deliberately vague and has therefore evolved without the need for formal amendment
- the Supreme Court has the power of judicial review (see Chapter 4)
- Americans have become cautious about tampering with the Constitution.

Typical mistake

The president has no formal role in passing constitutional amendments. Having been agreed by both houses of Congress, they are not subject to presidential approval and neither can the president veto them.

Exam tip

Note that a question about amending the US Constitution could require quite a substantial piece on the Supreme Court's power of judicial review.

Does the US Constitution still work?

Yes	No
<ul><li>Federalism has proved to be an excellent compromise between strong national government and state government diversity</li><li>The text has proved very adaptable to changes in American society</li><li>The demanding amendment process has usually prevented frequent and ill-conceived proposals for amendment</li><li>Rights and liberties of Americans have been protected</li><li>The Supreme Court's power of judicial review has made it even more adaptable through 'interpretative amendment'</li></ul>	<ul><li>The amendment process is too difficult, thereby making it well nigh impossible to amend parts no longer applicable or to add parts that a majority desires</li><li>Power of judicial review gives the Supreme Court too much power to 'amend' its meaning</li><li>The Constitution is too negative, giving too much power to those who oppose change</li><li>Some parts make little sense in today's society (e.g. the Electoral College)</li><li>Some parts don't work as the framers would have envisaged (e.g. war-making powers)</li></ul>

Now test yourself

TESTED

10 How can constitutional amendments be proposed?
11 How can constitutional amendments be ratified?
12 Give three advantages and three disadvantages of the amendment process.
13 What are the first ten amendments to the Constitution called?
14 Give two examples of subsequent constitutional amendments.
15 Give two reasons why the Constitution has been amended so rarely.

Answers on p. 107

The key principles of the Constitution

> **Separation of powers:** A theory of government whereby political power is distributed among the legislature, the executive and the judiciary, each acting both independently and interdependently.

The Constitution is based on three key principles:

1 Separation of powers.
2 Checks and balances.
3 Federalism.

Separation of powers

REVISED

To understand the principle of the **separation of powers** you need to realise that:

- the federal government is made up of three separate branches:
  - the legislature (Congress) – makes the laws
  - the executive (headed by the president) – carries out (executes) the laws
  - the judiciary (headed by the Supreme Court) – enforces and interprets the laws
- no one can belong to more than one of these branches at the same time – this is often referred to as 'the separation of personnel'

> **Typical mistake**
>
> Be careful not to confuse the word 'legislature' (a noun, as in 'the legislature') with the word 'legislative' (an adjective, as in 'the legislative process').

- the term is somewhat misleading as it's not the 'powers' that are separate but the institutions themselves
- therefore the Constitution created a governmental system made up of 'separated institutions, sharing powers'.

This sharing of powers is what the second of the Constitution's key principles – **checks and balances** – is about.

Checks and balances

Because the Constitution creates a system of separate institutions that share powers, each institution can check the powers of the others. The major checks possessed by each branch are set out in Table 1.5, along with some recent examples.

Checks and balances: A system of government that gives each branch – legislative, executive and judicial – the means to partially control the power exercised by the other branches.

Table 1.5 Examples of major checks and balances

Check by the president on Congress	
Veto a bill	Justice Against Sponsors of Terrorism Act (Obama, 2016)
Checks by the president on the federal courts	
Nominate judges	Neil Gorsuch (Trump, 2017)
Pardon	Of Sheriff Joe Arpaio (Trump, 2017)
Checks by Congress on the president	
Amend/delay/reject legislative proposals	American Health Care Act (2017) – Trump's attempt to repeal and replace 'Obamacare'
Override veto	Justice Against Sponsors of Terrorism Act (2016)
Refuse to approve appointments*	John Tower as Secretary of Defense (1989)
Refuse to ratify treaties*	Convention on the Rights of Persons with Disabilities (2012)
Impeachment and trial	Of President Bill Clinton (1998–99)
Checks by Congress on the federal courts	
Propose constitutional amendments	Proposed Federal Marriage Amendment (2015)
Refuse to approve appointments*	Merrick Garland to the Supreme Court (2016)
Check by the federal courts on Congress	
Declare law unconstitutional	Defense of Marriage Act (1996) in 2013
Check by the federal courts on the president	
Declare actions unconstitutional	Obama's recess appointments to the National Labor Relations Board (2014)

* Senate only.

Impeachment: A formal accusation of a serving federal official by a simple majority vote of the House of Representatives.

Federalism

The third key principle of the Constitution is **federalism**.

Nowhere is the word 'federal' or 'federalism' mentioned in the Constitution. It was written into the document in:

- the enumerated powers of the federal government
- the implied powers of the federal government
- the concurrent powers of the federal and state governments
- the Tenth Amendment.

The power relationship between the federal and state governments is also overseen by the Supreme Court through its power of judicial review.

> **Federalism:** A theory of government by which political power is divided between a national government and state governments, each having their own areas of substantive jurisdiction.

Federalism under George W. Bush

Republican presidents had traditionally sought to shrink the size and scope of the federal government. But in four policy areas, President George W. Bush (2001–09) presided over federal government expansion:

- education – 'No Child Left Behind' Act (2002)
- Medicare – a new prescription drug benefit for over-65s costing $400 billion in its first ten years
- Homeland security and defence – as a consequence of the 9/11 attacks in 2001
- economy and jobs – federal government takeover of two troubled privately owned, government-sponsored mortgage companies in 2008.

Federalism under Barack Obama

Democrat president Barack Obama (2009–17) moved away from Bush's focus on 'the war on terror' to focus on domestic policy in order to pursue his 'change' agenda. The Obama years saw an increase in federal government activity in such programmes as:

- an economic stimulus package (2009)
- the re-authorisation of the State Children's Health Insurance Program (S-CHIP) (2009)
- the expansion of Medicaid (health insurance programme for the poor)
- 'Obamacare' – Obama's flagship reform of the American healthcare system (2010).

Consequences of federalism

Federalism has consequences throughout US government and politics:

- Legal consequences – there is variation in state laws on such matters as the age at which people can marry, drive a car or have to attend school. Laws on the death penalty vary. There are federal and state courts.
- Policy consequences – states can act as policy laboratories, experimenting with new solutions to old problems. There is great variation between the states on such policies as healthcare provision, immigration, affirmative action and environmental protection.
- Consequences for elections – all elections are state based and run under state law.
- Consequences for political parties – political parties in America are essentially decentralised, state-based parties.
- Economic consequences – huge federal grants going to the states, as well as the complexity of the tax system because, for example, income tax is levied by both federal and some state governments.

● Regionalism – the regions of the South, the Midwest, the Northeast and the West have distinct cultures as well as racial, religious and ideological differences.

Now test yourself

TESTED

16 What are the three key principles of the Constitution?
17 Define the doctrine of the separation of powers.
18 Complete this quotation: 'The Constitution created a governmental system made up of separated _____ sharing _____.'
19 Give an example of each of the six sets of checks between the three branches of the federal government.
20 Give a definition of federalism.
21 How was federalism written into the Constitution?
22 Give two examples of the ways in which the size and scope of the federal government expanded under (a) George W. Bush and (b) Barack Obama.
23 Give three examples of the consequences of federalism.

Answers on pp. 107–08

Comparing the US and the UK constitutions

The origins of the two Constitutions

REVISED

The differences between the constitutions of the USA and the UK are largely reflective of the different cultures of these two countries. The US Constitution has been shaped by the expectations and fears of the late 18th century, such as:

● liberty
● individualism
● equality
● representative government
● limited government
● states' rights
● gun ownership
● a fear of state-organised religion.

The UK Constitution, meanwhile, has been shaped by a culture and society dominated by:

● an autocratic monarchy
● the hereditary principle
● the power of a landed aristocracy
● an established church
● a deferential working class
● a lack of social mobility.

The nature of the two Constitutions

REVISED

The two constitutions are different not only in origin but also in nature. They are structurally very different. The US Constitution is codified, yet it makes no mention at all of such important matters as:

● primary elections
● congressional committees
● the president's cabinet

- the Executive Office of the President
- the Supreme Court's power of judicial review.

Some things that to begin with were merely conventions – such as a two-term limit for the president – over time have become formalised in the codified document.

Whereas the UK Constitution is uncodified, much of it is written down in, for example:

- Acts of Parliament
- common law
- the works of Erskine May and Walter Bagehot.

Other important differences between the two constitutions are:

- The powers, requirements and rights in the US Constitution are entrenched whereas those in the UK Constitution are not.
- The US Constitution allows for much more popular and democratic participation than does the UK Constitution.
- The US Constitution establishes a separation of powers whereas the UK Constitution establishes more in the way of fused powers, especially between the executive and the legislature.
- Checks and balances are more significant in the US Constitution than in the UK Constitution.
- The US Constitution enshrines the principle of federalism whereas the UK Constitution enshrines the principle of devolution.

Table 1.6 summarises the main characteristics of the two Constitutions.

Table 1.6 Summary of comparisons between the US and UK constitutions

US Constitution	UK Constitution
Codified	Uncodified
Some (unwritten) conventions	Much is written
Entrenched	No entrenchment
More direct democratic participation	Emphasis on representative democracy
Separation of powers	Fusion of powers
Checks and balances	Fewer checks on power
Federalism	Devolution

Now test yourself

TESTED

24 Give three of the cultural factors that were important in the USA in the late 18th century that helped shape the US Constitution.
25 Give three of the cultural factors that helped shape the UK Constitution.
26 Give three parts of US government and politics not mentioned in the Constitution.
27 Name three places where one can find written parts of the UK Constitution.
28 Name three important differences between the nature of the US and the UK constitutions.

Answers on p. 108

Summary

You should now have an understanding of:
- why the US Constitution came to be written in its original form
- the significance of the process for constitutional amendment
- the link between separation of powers and checks and balances
- the way federalism works in the USA
- the similarities and differences of the US and UK constitutions and some of the reasons behind the differences.

Exam practice

Section A (comparative)

1 Examine the extent to which the US and UK constitutions are written and unwritten. [12]
2 Examine the provision of decentralisation in the US and UK constitutions. [12]

Section B (comparative)

In your answer you must consider the relevance of at least one comparative theory.
1 Analyse the significant differences between the US and UK constitutions in their provision of checks and balances. [12]
2 Analyse the differences between the US and UK constitutions in their provision of democratic participation. [12]

Section C (USA)

In your answer you must consider the stated view and the alternative to this view in a balanced way.
1 Evaluate the extent to which the US Constitution provides adequately for ongoing amendment. [30]
2 Evaluate the extent to which the states are dominated by the federal government. [30]

Answers and quick quiz online

ONLINE

2 Congress

The structure and composition of Congress

Congress is bicameral: it is made up of two houses – the House of Representatives and the Senate. This was part of the compromise made by the Founding Fathers at the Philadelphia Convention in 1787. Thus in the House of Representatives the number of members for each state is proportional to their population while in the Senate each state has two members regardless of population.

Other basic facts you need to know about Congress are that:
- the House has always been directly elected; the Senate only since 1914
- the number of representatives for each state in the House is reapportioned after every ten-yearly census
- senators represent the entire state; members of the House represent a sub-division of the state called a congressional district – except in those states with only one House member.

The composition of Congress is outlined in Table 2.1.

Table 2.1 Composition of Congress in outline

House of Representatives	Senate
<ul><li>Lower house</li><li>435 members</li><li>Represent a congressional district</li><li>Serve two-year terms</li><li>Must be at least 25 years old</li><li>Must have been a US citizen for at least seven years</li><li>Must be a resident of the state they represent</li></ul>	<ul><li>Upper house</li><li>100 members</li><li>Represent the entire state</li><li>Serve six-year terms</li><li>Must be at least 30 years old</li><li>Must have been a US citizen for at least nine years</li><li>Must be a resident of the state they represent</li></ul>

Even as recently as the 1980s, Congress was composed almost exclusively of white men. Only in the past two or three decades has the representation of women and members of ethnic minorities increased significantly. In January 2017:
- there were 104 women in Congress
- 83 were in the House and 21 in the Senate
- but that still means that only just over 15% of members of Congress were women
- of those 104 women, 78 were Democrats and just 26 Republicans.

In terms of ethnic minorities, in January 2017:
- 49 members of Congress (9%) were African-Americans – 46 in the House, 3 in the Senate
- 38 members of Congress (7%) were Hispanic/Latino – 34 in the House, 4 in the Senate
- 15 members of Congress (3%) were Asian – 12 in the House, 3 in the Senate.

In the country as a whole:

- 13.3% of the population are African-Americans
- 17.8% are Hispanic/Latino
- 5.6% are Asian.

Therefore all these racial groups are under-represented in Congress, especially Hispanic and Latino Americans.

In terms of party, both houses are dominated by the Republican and Democratic parties:

- Between 1993 and the end of 2018, the House had been controlled by the Democrats for 14 years and the Republicans for 12 years.
- During the same period, the Senate had been controlled by the Republicans for just over 14 years and by the Democrats for just over 11 years.
- Only two of Congress's 535 members belong to neither party – senators Bernie Sanders (Vermont) and Angus King (Maine) – but both almost always vote with the Democrats.

Now test yourself

TESTED

1 How many houses make up Congress?
2 How many members are there in each?
3 How is the membership of each house distributed among the 50 states?
4 How many women and members of racial minorities were in each house in January 2017?
5 To what extent do the two major parties dominate Congress?

Answers on pp. 108–09

The powers of Congress

Congress has ten formal, Constitutional powers, three of which are the most important because they are most frequently used.

1 Law making:
- both houses have equal power
- all bills must pass through all stages in both houses
- neither house can override the wishes of the other
- both houses must agree to the proposed law in exactly the same form before it can be sent to the president
- all money bills (tax bills) must begin in the House.

2 Overseeing the executive branch (investigation):
- an implied power of the Constitution
- oversight of executive departments and agencies – controls their budgets
- conducted in standing and select committees.

3 Confirming appointments:
- by the Senate only
- president's appointments to federal judiciary and executive
- the most important ones are those to the Supreme Court and to the president's cabinet
- simple majority required
- rarely rejected.

Typical mistake

Don't forget to say that confirming appointments is a power only of the Senate.

A second tier of powers includes:

1 Overriding the president's veto:
   ○ requires a two-thirds majority in both houses
   ○ is very difficult to achieve
   ○ President Obama vetoed 12 bills in his eight years – just one was overridden.
2 Ratifying treaties:
   ○ by the Senate only
   ○ requires two-thirds majority
   ○ rarely rejected.

The other powers of Congress are:

1 Initiating constitutional amendments.
2 **Impeaching**, trying and removing public officials.
3 Confirming an appointed vice president (used only in 1973 and 1974).
4 Declaring war (not used since 1941).
5 Electing the president (House) and vice president (Senate) if the Electoral College is deadlocked (not used since 1824).

> **Typical mistake**
>
> Say that a two-thirds majority is required but don't forget to say 'in both houses'.

> **Impeachment**: A formal accusation of a serving federal official by a simple majority vote of the House of Representatives.

> **Typical mistake**
>
> The term 'impeachment' is often misunderstood. It simply means to make a formal accusation against someone. It does not mean to remove someone from office, though it may lead to that.

> **Exam tip**
>
> If asked a question about the powers of Congress, it is better to focus on the most important ones rather than trying to cover all ten. So maybe cover the first three in detail, the next two with an example each and just mention one or two of the others.

Now test yourself

TESTED

6 What are the three main powers of Congress?
7 What does the term 'impeachment' mean?
8 What majorities are required to (a) confirm appointments, (b) override the president's veto and (c) ratify treaties?

Answers on p. 109

Comparing the House and the Senate

It is usually suggested that the Senate is **more powerful** than the House because of:
● its exclusive power to confirm appointments
● its exclusive power to ratify treaties.

It is usually suggested that the Senate is **more prestigious** than the House because:
● senators represent the entire state
● senators serve longer terms
● senators are one of only 100
● senators are more likely to chair a committee or sub-committee
● the Senate is seen as a recruiting pool for the presidency and the vice presidency (see Tables 2.2 and 2.3).

Therefore House members often seek election to the Senate but not the other way around – in 2017 there were 50 former House members in the Senate but no former senators in the House.

However, it must be remembered that both chambers are equal in:
● passing legislation
● conducting oversight of the executive
● initiating constitutional amendments
● fulfilling a representative function
● their level of salaries.

Exam tip

Don't forget the ways in which both chambers are equal.

Table 2.2 Serving and former senators who ran as presidential candidates in 2016

Republicans	Democrats
Ted Cruz	Hillary Clinton
Rand Paul	Bernie Sanders
Marco Rubio	Jim Webb
Rick Santorum	
Lindsey Graham	

Table 2.3 Former senators who served as vice president: 1977–2017

Vice president	Party	Dates in office
Walter Mondale	Democratic	1977–81
Dan Quayle	Republican	1989–93
Al Gore	Democratic	1993–2001
Joe Biden	Democratic	2009–17
Mike Pence	Republican	2017–

Now test yourself

TESTED

9 What are the two important exclusive powers of the Senate?
10 Give three reasons why the Senate is regarded as more prestigious than the House.
11 Give three ways in which the Senate and House are equal.
12 Give two examples of serving or former senators who ran for the presidency in 2016.
13 Name two recent vice presidents who had previously served in the Senate.

Answers on p. 109

The committee system

The four most important types of committee in Congress are:
1 Standing committees.
2 House Rules Committee.
3 Conference committees.
4 Select committees.

Typical mistake

Watch that you don't misspell the word 'committee' – two 'm's, two 't's and two 'e's.

Standing committees

Standing committees:

- exist in both houses (e.g. House Judiciary Committee, Senate Foreign Relations Committee)
- are mostly divided into sub-committees
- have around 18 members in the Senate, around 30–40 members in the House
- have three main functions:
  - ○ conducting the committee stage of bills
  - ○ conducting investigations
  - ○ beginning the process of confirming appointments (Senate committees only).

The party balance of each committee reflects the party balance of the respective chamber.

> **Standing committee**: A permanent, policy specialist committee of Congress playing key roles in both legislation and investigation.

Conducting the committee stage of bills

Committees:

- scrutinise bills in their particular policy area
- hold hearings on the bill
- call witnesses to give evidence at their hearings
- have full power of amendment.

Conducting investigations

Committees:

- investigate issues within their particular policy area
- investigate perceived problems, crises, policy failures
- oversee relevant executive departments and agencies
- call witnesses to appear at hearings
- can be high profile and influential.

Beginning confirmation process (Senate only)

Committees:

- hold hearings on executive branch appointments made by the president within their particular policy area
- vote on whether or not to recommend the full Senate to confirm a nominee (see Table 2.4).

The Senate Judiciary Committee also considers all presidential nominations to the federal judiciary.

Table 2.4 Standing committee votes on selected Trump cabinet officers, 2017

Post	Nominee	Standing committee	Vote
Secretary of Defense	Jim Mattis	Armed Services	26–1
Secretary of State	Rex Tillerson	Foreign Relations	11–10
Secretary of the Treasury	Steve Mnuchin	Finance	11–0*
Attorney General	Jeff Sessions	Judiciary	11–9

* All Democrat members of the committee boycotted the vote.

House Rules Committee

REVISED

This committee:
- is one of the standing committees in the House
- but performs a totally different function from the others
- is responsible for prioritising bills coming from the committee stage on to the floor of the House for their debate and votes
- gives a 'rule' to a bill setting out the rules of debate, stating whether or not further amendments are permitted
- has just 13 members – 9 from the majority party, 4 from the minority party
- is highly influential: 'the legislative gate-keeper' of the House.

Conference committees

REVISED

These committees:
- are ad hoc (temporary)
- are made up of members from both chambers
- are set up to reconcile differences between House and Senate versions of a bill
- need to make compromises agreeable to a majority of both houses
- are important because they will often draw up the final version of the bill – but their compromise version must be passed by a majority vote in both houses.

> **Typical mistake**
>
> Although a conference committee has members from both chambers, don't confuse them with joint committees, which are mainly used for administrative purposes only.

Select committees

REVISED

These committees:
- are also known as 'special' or 'investigative' committees
- are mostly ad hoc
- are used when an investigation does not fall within the policy area of one standing committee, or when the investigation is likely to be particularly time-consuming (see Table 2.5).

Table 2.5 Summary of the importance of congressional committees

Type of committee	They are important because they:
Standing committees	• are regarded as policy specialists • conduct the committee stage of bills, which comes *before* the main debate in either chamber • conduct high-profile investigations • (in the Senate) begin the confirmation process of numerous presidential nominations
House Rules Committee	• control the passage of bills from the committees to the floor in the House • decide the terms of debate for each bill – for example, whether or not amendments are permitted • are seen as the 'gate-keeper' of the legislative process in the House
Conference committees	• come right at the end of the legislative process • have almost life or death power over a bill • often write what will be the final version of the bill
Select committees	• conduct high-profile and often long-running investigations

14 Name three different types of congressional committee.
15 How many members typically make up a standing committee in each house?
16 How is the party balance of each standing committee decided?
17 What functions do standing committees have?
18 Give an example of a standing committee vote on President Trump's cabinet nominees.
19 What does the House Rules Committee do?
20 What is the function of a conference committee?
21 Why would a select committee be set up?

Answers on p. 109

Congress and legislation

The legislative process in Congress is best thought of in six stages, as shown in Table 2.6.

Table 2.6 The six stages of the legislative process in Congress

Stage	What happens
1 Introduction	• A formality • Between 10,000 and 14,000 bills introduced in a typical Congress (two years) • Only about 2–4% of those will become law
2 Committee stage	• The most important stage • Comes before the full chamber has debated the bill • Conducted by the relevant standing committee (see above) • Committees hold hearings on bills • Have full power of amendment • After hearings, committee writes report, which recommends future action • However, most bills never get any further
3 Timetabling	• In the House, by the House Rules Committee (see above) • In the Senate, by unanimous consent agreement
4 Floor debate and vote	• Further amendments are possible • Votes are taken: either voice votes or recorded votes • In the Senate, a **filibuster** is possible, which can be ended by a successful cloture motion
5 Conference committee	• Used to reconcile the differences between the House and Senate versions of the bill (see above) • But this work is now often done behind the scenes by an ad hoc, leadership-driven group

6 Presidential action	• The president has four options:
	  – sign the bill into law
	  – leave the bill on his desk (it becomes law within 10 working days)
	  – **presidential veto** (Congress may override with two-thirds majorities in both houses)
	  – **pocket veto** (usable only at the end of the legislative session)

Filibuster: A device by which one or more senators can delay action on a bill or any other matter by debating it at length or through other obstructive actions.

Presidential veto: The president's power under Article II of the Constitution to return a bill to Congress unsigned, along with the reasons for his objection.

Pocket veto: A veto power exercised by the president at the end of a legislative session whereby bills not signed are lost.

On average, only between 3% and 4% of bills that are introduced into Congress are actually passed into law. So that raises the question: 'How effective is Congress in fulfilling its legislative function?' There are arguments on both sides.

Debate

How effective is Congress in fulfilling its legislative function?

It is effective because:	It is not effective because:
• the process is deliberately designed to be complicated and to weed out unpopular legislation • an average of 300 new Acts of Congress signed into law every two years is still quite a lot – especially considering all the new laws that are passed by the 50 state legislatures • 'limited government' is a founding principle of American government – a belief that government should act only when it is essential • Congress has passed some significant pieces of legislation in recent decades relating to gun violence, free trade, education, campaign finance, economic recovery and healthcare reform	• the procedures of Congress often mean that the will of the majority can be frustrated by a well-organised minority (e.g. power of committee chairs, filibustering, need for super-majorities) • the small-population states are over-represented in the Senate • the two-yearly election cycle in the House means members spend too much time fundraising and campaigning and not enough time on legislation • Congress spends a lot of time debating and voting on bills of minor importance (e.g. allowing the Postal Service to issue a commemorative stamp)

Now test yourself   TESTED

22 Why is the committee stage of a bill so important?
23 What is a filibuster?
24 What options does the president have when a bill is sent to him?
25 Explain the terms (a) presidential veto and (b) pocket veto.
26 How can Congress override a presidential veto?

Answers on p. 109

Congress and oversight

Congress carries out its **oversight** function through:
● standing committee hearings
● the subpoena of documents and testimony
● the Senate's power to confirm appointments
● the Senate's power to ratify treaties.

Because there are no executive branch members present in the legislature, oversight work is conducted mostly in the standing committees of both houses.

Oversight: Congressional review and investigation of the activities of the executive branch of government.

It is effective because:	It is not effective because:
● appearances by senior members of the executive branch at congressional committee hearings are a real check on their power ● oversight hearings often receive high levels of media coverage ● presidential nominations to the executive and judicial branches can be dealt death blows by Senate standing committees ● committee members are policy experts in their own fields and therefore can ask searching questions	● members of the president's party may ask 'soft ball' questions during hearings ● members of the opposition party may indulge in partisan point-scoring rather than effective oversight ● committees rarely vote to reject presidential nominees to the executive and judicial branches ● lengthy hearings don't necessarily result in effective oversight (e.g. House Republican hearings on terrorist attack in Benghazi, 2012)

Now test yourself

TESTED

27 What is meant by the term 'oversight'?
28 Give two ways in which Congress carries out this function.
29 Why is oversight carried out in committees rather than in the chambers?

Answers on p. 109

Congress and representation

The models through which legislators represent their constituents are outlined in Table 2.7.

Table 2.7 Representation in Congress

How legislators represent their constituents	Who the legislators are
The trustee model: ● legislator makes decisions on behalf of constituents ● legislator uses their 'mature judgement' The delegate model: ● legislator makes decisions to reflect their constituents' views	Whether legislators are representative of their constituents in terms of: ● gender ● race ● age ● socio-economic class ● previous occupation ● education

Exam tip

If answering a question on 'representation' in Congress, always make sure that you clearly define the term, explaining the differences in Table 2.7.

Models of representation

REVISED

There are two models of **representation** that you need to understand in terms of *how* legislators represent their constituents: the trustee model and the delegate model.

The trustee model

● As advocated by James Madison and Edmund Burke.
● The legislator makes decisions on behalf of their constituents – the legislator acts as a 'trustee'.

Representation: Either how legislators represent their constituents or who the legislators are and whether they are 'representative' of constituents in terms of, for example, gender and race.

- The legislator will decide based on their 'mature judgement'.
- Critics see this as elitist.

The delegate model

- The legislator decides in accordance with the views of a majority of their constituents.
- The legislator does not exercise their own judgement – they are 'delegated' to act in a way that is in accordance with their constituents' views.
- This is linked with the principle of popular sovereignty – where the views of 'the people' are paramount.
- It is seen by supporters as more populist and democratic.

Most members of Congress will probably see their representative role as a blend of both models, though House members – subject to a two-yearly election cycle – will tend to lean more to putting a higher premium on constituents' views.

Engagement with constituents

Members of Congress engage with their constituents through many different methods and channels, including:

- holding party and town hall meetings
- conducting 'surgeries' with individual constituents
- making visits around the state/district
- appearing on local radio phone-ins
- taking part in interviews with local media
- addressing various groups in their state/district, e.g. chambers of commerce, Rotary clubs
- using e-mail and social media.

> **Debate**
>
> **How effective is Congress at fulfilling its representative function?**
>
> | It is effective because of: | It is not effective because: |
> | --- | --- |
> | <ul><li>the frequency of elections (especially in the House)</li><li>the constitutional requirement that members of Congress must reside in the state they represent (plus the locality rule for House members in many states)</li><li>the number of ways constituents can now share their views with members of Congress</li></ul> | <ul><li>constituents' views on many issues are very divided</li><li>many members of Congress see themselves more as a 'trustee' than a 'delegate'</li><li>in today's era of hyper-partisanship, following the party line often trumps constituency representation as the main cue in voting</li></ul> |

Now test yourself

TESTED ☐

30 Explain the two different interpretations of the word 'representation'.
31 Explain the difference between the trustee and delegate models of representation.
32 Give four ways in which members of Congress engage with constituents.

Answers on p. 109

Voting in Congress

There are six main factors that affect voting in Congress. We have just considered one of those – constituents – so now we consider the other five.

Political party

There has been much increased party unity within congressional parties during the past two decades.

However, parties have few, if any, incentives or disincentives to encourage party-line voting.

Those members who stray from the party line may find themselves faced by a primary challenger in the next election cycle.

The administration

The president, vice president, senior members of the White House staff and the president's congressional liaison staff all lobby members of Congress to support them on key votes.

Cabinet members lobby in their respective policy areas.

Success for the administration depends on a number of variables:
- the size of the president's mandate at the last election
- the president's current approval rating in the country
- the first term – this tends to be more successful than the second term
- the president's persuasive skills and relationship with his own party in Congress.

Pressure groups

Pressure groups try to influence how members of Congress vote:
- through direct contact with key members (e.g. at committee hearings)
- by generating public support for the positions they favour
- by organising rallies, demonstrations, etc.
- through fundraising and campaigning.

Colleagues and staff

Colleagues and staff are:
- the same state delegation (in the House)
- relevant committee members
- respected senior members
- senior members of staff (e.g. chief of staff, legislative assistants).

Personal beliefs

Personal beliefs have an influence on voting, especially on moral issues or matters affecting members' personal philosophy.

Exam tip

Always remember that factors will vary from one member to another and from one vote to another. Also, most votes will be a result of a number of factors, not just one.

Now test yourself

33 Give three important factors that may determine the way members of Congress vote.
34 Give three examples of people/groups who may lobby members of Congress on behalf of the administration.

Answers on p. 109

Parties in Congress

The two major parties dominate Congress:
- Almost all members are either Democrats or Republicans.
- The major parties control all leadership positions.

The two major parties have become more ideologically cohesive during the past two decades:
- an era of 'hyper-**partisanship**' (Brownstein)
- greater unity within the parties, especially in the House (see Figure 2.1)
- more distinct conflicts between the parties
- big-ticket items tend to pass on strictly party-line votes (e.g. President Trump's tax cuts in December 2017 received no Democrat votes in either house)
- few 'centrists' are left in Congress.

This makes bipartisanship and cooperation 'across the aisle' much more difficult than it was.

It often leads to **gridlock**.

This all represents a significant change from just a few decades ago when parties in Congress were not that important because:
- the Democrats and Republicans were at times almost indistinguishable from one another
- both contained 'liberals' and 'conservatives'
- a typical vote in Congress used to be one group of Democrats and Republicans voting against another group of Democrats and Republicans
- 'party unity' was very low, especially in the House (see Figure 2.1)
- both contained so-called 'centrists', who frequently participated in bipartisan votes
- the emphasis was then more on individual members and sub-groups of the parties rather than on the parties themselves
- the role of the party leadership was not that important or influential.

Partisanship: A situation where members of one party regularly group together to oppose members of another party, characterised by strong party discipline and little cooperation between the parties.

Gridlock: Failure to get action on policy proposals and legislation in Congress. Gridlock is thought to be exacerbated by divided government and partisanship.

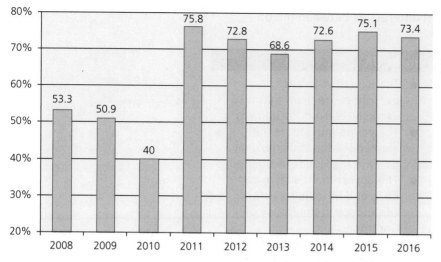

Figure 2.1 Party unity votes: House of Representatives, 2008–16

Source: www.brookings.edu. Data indicate the percentage of all roll call votes on which a majority of Democrats voted against a majority of Republicans.

Debate

Do parties play an important role in Congress?

Yes, they do play an important role because:	No, they do not play an important role because:
● leadership in Congress is run by the parties ● committees in Congress are organised by the parties ● with increased partisanship, party discipline is much stronger in Congress than it used to be ● party is an important determinant of voting in Congress ● it is almost impossible to be elected to Congress without being a major party candidate	● views of constituents can often outweigh party considerations – especially for House members ● parties have no control over candidate selection ● both parties are made up of ideological factions that compete with party cohesion ● the executive branch has few 'sticks or carrots' by which to incentivise party discipline ● congressional leadership, likewise, is fairly impotent in the face of opposition

---

Now test yourself   TESTED ☐

35 In what two ways do the two major parties dominate Congress?
36 Name two consequences of the two major parties having become more ideologically cohesive.
37 Explain the terms (a) partisanship and (b) gridlock.
38 What has happened to the number of 'centrists' in Congress?
39 Explain what the data in Figure 2.1 show.

Answers on p. 110

Comparing Congress with the UK Parliament

The differences between the US Congress and the UK Parliament are mainly the result of the fundamental structural differences between the two systems of government (see Table 2.8). Table 2.9 compares the similarities and differences.

Table 2.8 Summary of the structural differences between the US Congress and the UK Parliament

In the US	In the UK
• Members of Congress are not permitted to hold a post in the executive at the same time • The president and vice president are elected independently from members of Congress • Executive branch members can be removed by Congress only through impeachment • The president has few 'sticks and carrots' to encourage party discipline	• The executive branch personnel are drawn almost exclusively from Parliament • The prime minister is the elected leader of the largest party in the House of Commons • The government's term can be ended by losing a vote of confidence in the House of Commons • The prime minister can encourage party discipline through the power of patronage

Table 2.9 Comparing Congress and Parliament: similarities and differences

Similarities	Differences
Both are bicameral	Congress: both houses elected Parliament: only one house elected
Different parties may control each house	Congress: two equal houses Parliament: lower house dominates
President/Prime minister's party may not control both houses	Congress: only two parties represented Parliament: multiple parties, especially in the House of Commons
Both houses in both institutions have a role in passing legislation and in oversight of the executive	Congress: executive branch excluded Parliament: executive branch included
Much work is done away from the chambers in committees	Terms of office: two years in the House of Representatives; five years in the House Commons; six years in the Senate
Oversight function is conducted by the standing committees in Congress and by the select committees of the House of Commons	Size of upper houses: Senate – 100; House of Lords – around 800 (lower house is also significantly larger in the UK)
All elections are on a first-past-the-post system	Senate has oversight powers unknown to the House of Lords (e.g. confirmation of appointments)
	Each American has three representatives in Congress (two in the Senate, one in the House); each British person has only one representative in Parliament

Exam practice answers and quick quizzes at **www.hoddereducation.co.uk/myrevisionnotesdownloads**

Composition of Congress and Parliament

The differences between Congress and Parliament in terms of composition are mainly the result of the different structural and cultural backgrounds of the two nations (see Table 2.10).

Table 2.10 Structural and cultural differences affecting the composition of Congress and Parliament

In Congress	In Parliament
• The institution reflects the federal structure of the USA • Members of both houses represent states (Senate) or part of a state (House) • The directly elected upper chamber reflects the principle of democratic participation	• The institution reflects the unitary/devolved structure of the UK • MPs represent the historic counties, cities and towns of the UK • The hereditary/appointed upper chamber reflects a nation in which the landed gentry and the established church were dominant

Powers and functions of Congress and Parliament

Legislation

In terms of dealing with legislation, there are significant differences between Congress and Parliament, mostly resulting from the structural differences between the two systems – one a presidential system based on the separation of powers, the other a parliamentary system based on a fusion of powers (see Table 2.11).

Table 2.11 Legislative function of Congress and Parliament compared

In Congress	In Parliament
No government programme of legislation exists	A government programme of legislation dominates the agenda
Level of party discipline is lower	There are higher levels of party discipline
Thousands of bills are introduced in any one session	Limited number of bills are introduced in any one session
Individual members introduce numerous pieces of legislation	Individual members introduce few pieces of legislation
Few of these bills are passed into law	Most bills are passed into law
Committee stage comes before the debate in the chamber	Committee stage comes after the Second Reading debate in the chamber
Standing committees are permanent and policy specialist	Standing committees are non-permanent and non-specialist
Bills are usually considered by both houses concurrently	Bills are considered by the two houses consecutively
Two chambers have equal powers	Lower chamber dominates
President has significant veto power	The Royal Assent is no longer withheld

Oversight

In terms of dealing with oversight of the executive branch, Congress and Parliament again have significant differences resulting from the structural differences between the two systems (see Table 2.12).

Table 2.12 Methods of oversight in Congress and Parliament compared

In Congress	In Parliament
• Standing committee hearings • Select committee hearings • Confirmation of appointments (Senate) • Ratification of treaties (Senate) • Impeachment, trial, removal from office	• Question time (including Prime Minister's Question Time) • Select committee hearings • Liaison Committee hearings • Correspondence with ministers • Tabling of early day motions • Policy debates • Office of the Ombudsman • Votes of no confidence

Representation

In terms of fulfilling their representative function, the differences between members of Congress and members of the House of Commons can best be understood along the lines of the rational choice approach, which highlights the way these two sets of legislators operate according to their self-interest. Members of the Senate, the House of Representatives and the House of Commons tend to fulfil their representative functions by considering who controls their electoral destiny – both at the nomination stage and in the election itself (see Table 2.13).

Table 2.13 Factors likely to influence members of Congress and members of the House of Commons in fulfilling their representative function

In Congress	In House of Commons
• Members must face voters every two (House) or six (Senate) years • Nomination is in the hands of ordinary voters in the primary	• Members must face voters at least every five years • Nomination is in the hands of the local party members

Comparing the two lower chambers

REVISED

Both the House of Representatives and the House of Commons are directly elected, but that is about as far as the similarities go. The differences are numerous (see Table 2.14).

Table 2.14 The two lower chambers compared

House of Representatives	House of Commons
Members serve maximum term of two years	Members serve maximum term of five years
Term fixed by the Constitution (entrenched)	Term fixed by Act of Parliament, but with provisos
Only two parties represented	Eight parties currently represented
No executive branch members	Includes executive branch members
Shares equal legislative power with upper chamber	Has ultimate legislative power on most matters
Members represent numerically equal electoral districts	Members represent numerically unequal electoral districts
Focus of the legislative process is in the standing committees	Focus of the legislative process is on the floor of the chamber
Committee stage comes before floor debate	Committee stage comes after floor debate
Legislative committees are permanent and policy specialist	Legislative committees are ad hoc
Oversight of the executive takes place only in committee rooms	Oversight of the executive takes place both in the chamber and in committee rooms
The Speaker is a partisan figure	The Speaker is a neutral umpire of debate
Senior members 'retire' to the upper chamber	Members seek elevation to the upper chamber to advance their political careers

Comparing the two upper chambers

REVISED

When it comes to the two upper chambers, the differences are so great that comparison becomes quite difficult (see Table 2.15).

Table 2.15 The two upper chambers compared

Senate	House of Lords
Directly elected (since 1914)	By appointment or heredity
100 members	Around 800 sitting members
Members serve six-year terms	Most serve for life
Dominated by only two parties	Includes a significant number of members who are non-partisan (cross-benchers, bishops)
Has equal legislative power with lower chamber	Essentially has only a delaying power over legislation
Has power to confirm executive and judicial appointments	Has no power to confirm executive and judicial appointments
Has power to ratify treaties	Has no power to ratify treaties
Seen as a recruiting ground for presidents and vice presidents	Seen as retirement post for long-serving politicians
Has equal oversight powers with lower house	Oversight powers seen as less important than those of the lower house

Now test yourself

40 Give two structural differences between Congress and Parliament.
41 Give four similarities and four differences between Congress and Parliament.
42 Give two structural/cultural differences that affect the composition of Congress and Parliament.
43 Give four differences in the ways that Congress and Parliament deal with legislation.
44 Name four methods Congress and Parliament use to perform their oversight function.
45 Give four ways in which the House of Representatives and the House of Commons differ.
46 Give four ways in which the Senate and the House of Lords differ.

Answers on p. 110

Summary

You should now have an understanding of:
● the structure and composition of Congress
● the powers of Congress
● the importance of congressional committees
● the effectiveness of Congress in legislation, oversight and representation
● voting in Congress
● the role of parties in Congress
● the similarities and differences between Congress and the UK Parliament

Exam practice

Section A (comparative)

1 Examine the ways in which the US Senate and the UK House of Lords differ.   [12]
2 Examine the ways in which the US Congress and the UK Parliament pass legislation.   [12]

Section B (comparative)

In your answer you must consider the relevance of at least one comparative theory.
1 Analyse the ways in which the US Congress and the UK Parliament perform their oversight function.
                                                                                                [12]
2 Analyse the ways in which members of the US House of Representatives and the UK House of Commons perform their representative function.   [12]

Section C (USA)

In your answer you must consider the stated view and the alternative to this view in a balanced way.
1 Evaluate the extent to which the Senate is more powerful and prestigious than the House.   [30]
2 Evaluate the extent to which Congress is an effective legislative body.   [30]

Answers and quick quiz online

3 The presidency

The formal powers of the president

The Constitution gives the president nine powers, outlined in Table 3.1.

Table 3.1 **The nine powers of the president**

1 Propose legislation	<ul><li>Often uses the annual State of the Union Address to Congress</li><li>For example, Obama (2013): job creation, immigration reform, increase in federal minimum wage</li><li>This power also includes submission of annual budget</li></ul>
2 Sign legislation	<ul><li>May hold bill-signing ceremony to claim credit</li><li>For example, Trump tax cuts (2017)</li></ul>
3 Veto legislation	<ul><li>Even the threat of a veto is a significant power</li><li>When used, the president usually prevails – Obama won on 11 out of 12 (2009–17)</li></ul>
4 Act as chief executive	<ul><li>In charge of running the executive branch</li><li>Assisted by cabinet: department and agency heads</li><li>Executive Office of the President (EXOP)</li></ul>
5 Nominate executive branch officials	<ul><li>Department and agency heads</li><li>For example, Trump appointed Mike Pompeo as Secretary of State (2018)</li></ul>
6 Nominate federal judges	<ul><li>Including Supreme Court justices</li><li>For example, Trump appointed Neil Gorsuch (2017)</li></ul>
7 Act as commander-in-chief	<ul><li>By December 2017, the USA still had around 26,000 troops in Afghanistan, Iraq and Syria</li></ul>
8 Negotiate treaties	<ul><li>Symbolises the peace-making role alongside the commander-in-chief role</li></ul>
9 Pardon	<ul><li>Controversial power, especially when used to benefit close friends and supporters</li></ul>

Now test yourself

TESTED

1 What powers does the president have concerning legislation?
2 What is the president's annual address to Congress called?
3 What appointment powers does the president have? Give two examples.
4 What foreign policy powers does the president have?

Answers on p. 110

Exam tip

If asked about the powers of the president in an exam question, you will need to group powers together so as not to have too many points to deal with, e.g.
1. legislative powers (1–3);
2. executive powers (4);
3. appointment powers (5–6);
4. foreign policy powers (7–8).

The vice president

The vice president is elected on a joint ticket with the president, e.g. Donald Trump and Mike Pence in 2016.

The president can fill a vacancy in the vice presidency by appointment, as has occurred twice (Gerald Ford in 1973; Nelson Rockefeller in 1974). This appointment must be confirmed by Congress.

The Constitution gives the vice president five powers – see Table 3.2.

Table 3.2 The five powers of the vice president

1 Presiding officer of the Senate	● Chairs debates (but usually this is done by junior members of the majority party)
2 Voting in the case of a tied vote in the Senate	● For example, Pence broke a 50–50 tied vote to confirm Betsy DeVos as secretary of education (2017)
3 Counting the Electoral College votes after the presidential election	● Pence will count the Electoral College votes in January 2021 following the 2020 election
4 Becoming president in the event of the death, resignation or removal of the president	● Has occurred on nine occasions ● Vice President Gerald Ford became president when President Nixon resigned (1974)
5 Becoming acting president if the president is declared, or declares himself, disabled (by Twenty-fifth Amendment)	● Vice President Dick Cheney twice became acting president while President George W. Bush underwent exploratory surgery

It is clearly the second and fourth of these powers that give the vice president the most potential significance.

Now test yourself

TESTED

5 How is the vice president elected?
6 What happens if the vice presidency falls vacant?
7 What are the two most significant powers of the vice president?

Answers on p. 110

The cabinet

The **cabinet** is not mentioned in the Constitution.
● Article II states the president 'may require the opinion in writing' of the heads of each executive department.
● Richard Fenno stated that the cabinet has become 'institutionalised by usage alone' – it's used because it's used.
● It is an advisory and co-ordinating, not a decision-making, group.

> **Cabinet**: The advisory group selected by the president to aid him in making decisions and coordinating the work of the federal government.

Membership and appointment

REVISED

The heads of the 15 executive departments are traditionally members of the cabinet, plus others whom the president designates as having cabinet rank (e.g. US Trade Representative).
● In 2017, Trump had eight such additional members, plus the vice president.
● It is difficult to recruit cabinet members from incumbent members of Congress as they must resign from Congress.
● Cabinet members are drawn from former members of Congress, state governors, big-city mayors, academia, etc.
● They tend to be policy specialists.
● Appointments must be confirmed by a majority vote in the Senate.
● Presidents like to appoint a cabinet that is balanced in terms of:
  ○ gender
  ○ race

> **Exam tip**
>
> The quotation from Fenno is just the kind of scholarly quotation that examiners like to see in your essay.

> **Typical mistake**
>
> Don't use the term 'cabinet ministers' for the USA. The correct term is 'cabinet officers'.

  ○ region
  ○ age
  ○ ideology.
- The cabinet often looks like the president in terms of these criteria (e.g. the Trump cabinet is mainly white, male, older, wealthy business executives).

Meetings

REVISED

Frequency of meetings varies from one president to another.
- Trump held nine in 2017 (well above the recent average).
- Presidents tend to hold fewer cabinet meetings as their presidency progresses.
- Cabinet meetings can fulfil different functions for the president:
  ○ engender team spirit
  ○ promote collegiality
  ○ exchange information
  ○ debate/promote policy, especially 'big-ticket' items.
- Cabinet officers may see meetings as a chance to:
  ○ get to know colleagues
  ○ resolve interdepartmental disputes
  ○ speak to the president.

Debate

Is the president's cabinet important?

Yes	No
● It contains some of the most important people in the executive branch (e.g. secretary of state, secretary of defense) ● All the heads of the 15 executive departments are automatically members ● The president always chairs the meetings ● Cabinet meetings can fulfil a number of important functions, both for the president and for cabinet officers ● Some presidents hold frequent meetings (e.g. Reagan, Trump)	● Article II of the Constitution vests 'all executive power' in the president ● There is no doctrine of collective responsibility ● The members are neither the president's equals nor his political rivals ● The president often views members of his cabinet with some suspicion because of their divided loyalties ● EXOP is the main source of advice-giving for the president

Now test yourself

TESTED

8 Give a definition of the president's cabinet.
9 Why do so few cabinet members come from Congress?
10 Where else do presidents look when recruiting their cabinet?
11 In what ways do presidents seek to appoint a balanced cabinet?
12 What functions can cabinet meetings serve for the president?
13 What functions can cabinet meetings serve for cabinet members?

Answers on p. 110

Exam tip

When debating the importance of the cabinet, you may need to distinguish between the cabinet as a group (i.e. the cabinet meeting) and cabinet officers as individuals.

The Executive Office of the President

The **Executive Office of the President (EXOP)** was established in 1939 with just four offices.

- By 2017 EXOP was made up of 12 offices.
- The number has increased because the number of policy areas that the president must address has increased.
- Key EXOP personnel work in the West Wing (where the Oval Office is located).
- The three most important offices within the Executive Office of the President are the White House Office, the Office of Management and Budget (OMB) and the National Security Council (NSC).

> **Executive Office of the President (EXOP)**: The umbrella term for the top staff agencies in the White House that assist the president in carrying out the major responsibilities of office.

White House Office

Also known as the White House Staff, this includes the president's most trusted aides and advisers.

It is made up of more than 30 different offices, such as:
- Office of Legislative Affairs
- Office of Cabinet Affairs.

It acts as liaison between the White House and the vast federal bureaucracy.
- Staff are meant to act as neutral 'honest brokers', not partisan policy-makers.
- It is headed by the White House chief of staff:
  - the door-keeper of the Oval Office
  - decides for the president whom he sees, what he reads, who speaks to him on the phone
  - should act as someone who sometimes takes the blame for the president if things go wrong
  - potentially the most powerful person in the White House after the president.

> **Typical mistake**
>
> EXOP is not an office *alongside* the White House Office, OMB, NSC, etc. It is the umbrella organisation that is *made up of* the White House Office, OMB, NSC, etc.

Office of Management and Budget

The OMB is headed by the OMB director.
- The appointment requires Senate confirmation.
- The OMB has three principal functions:
  - to advise the president on the allocation of federal funds in the annual budget
  - to oversee the spending of all federal departments and agencies
  - to act as a clearing house for all legislative and regulatory initiatives coming from the president.

National Security Council (NSC)

The main function of the NSC is to help the president coordinate foreign, security and defence policy.
- It is headed by the national security adviser.
- The NSC coordinates information coming to the president from:
  - the State Department
  - the Defense Department

○ the Central Intelligence Agency (CIA)
○ the joint chiefs of staff
○ US ambassadors around the world.
● It is important that the NSC acts as an 'honest broker', a facilitator, not a policy promoter.

> **Exam tip**
>
> When preparing for your exam, use an internet search engine to find out something that one of these three offices within EXOP has been recently involved in. Good example material!

The problem of EXOP–cabinet rivalries

REVISED

In many administrations, rivalries break out between those who work in EXOP and those who work in the cabinet. Rivalries can develop for various reasons:

1 While EXOP members work in or near the West Wing, cabinet members often work some geographic distance from the White House.
2 While key EXOP members may see the president on a regular basis, some members of the cabinet rarely get to see the president – and certainly not one on one.
3 Therefore, while EXOP members often know what the president wants from day to day, cabinet members may feel out of the loop.
4 While EXOP members work only for the president, cabinet members have divided loyalties – to the president, but also to Congress, to their bureaucracy and to client pressure groups.
5 EXOP staff therefore often regard cabinet members as being disloyal.

Now test yourself

TESTED

14 What is the Executive Office of the President (EXOP)?
15 How many offices made up EXOP in 2017?
16 What is the main function of the White House Office?
17 Give three key roles of the White House chief of staff.
18 Give two functions of the Office of Management and Budget (OMB).
19 What is the main function of the National Security Council (NSC)?
20 Name three organisations/groups of people from whom the NSC coordinates information.
21 Give three reasons why rivalries can develop between EXOP and members of the president's cabinet.

Answers on pp. 110–11

The president's relations with Congress

What is the president trying to get Congress to do?
● Pass his legislative proposals.
● Sustain his vetoes.
● Confirm his executive and judicial nominations (Senate only).
● Ratify his treaties (Senate only).

Why does a president need to persuade Congress to support him?

> **Exam tip**
>
> If you are answering a question about *how* the president persuades/works with members of Congress, don't forget to begin your answer by explaining *why* he needs to persuade them to support him.

- The powers he has are checked by Congress (see Table 3.3).
- His party may control only one house of Congress, or neither.
- Members of Congress have other loyalties than to the president, especially to their constituents and to powerful lobbyists.
- Members of Congress are elected separately from the president.
- The president has few 'sticks and carrots' (disincentives and incentives) to encourage members of Congress to support him.

Table 3.3 Powers of the president and checks by Congress

Powers of the president	Checks by Congress
Propose legislation	Amend, delay, reject the president's legislative proposals
Veto legislation	Override the veto
Nominate executive branch officials	Senate has the power to confirm or reject
Nominate federal judges	Senate has the power to confirm or reject
Negotiate treaties	Senate has the power to ratify or reject
Commander-in-chief of the armed forces	Declare war/power of the purse
Act as chief executive	Investigation, impeachment, trial, removal from office

Whom does the president use to help him get Congress's support?
- The vice president.
- The Office of Legislative Affairs (part of the White House Office).
- Cabinet officers.
- Party leadership in Congress.

What 'perks' can the president use to help win the support of members of Congress?
- Phone calls.
- Support legislation important to a member of Congress.
- Invitations – social or political – to the White House.
- Campaign for them (only for members from the president's party).
- Go on TV to appeal directly to voters and ask them to contact their members of Congress and tell them to support him.

What success have recent presidents enjoyed in Congress?
- Success can be measured by the presidential support score – an annual statistic that measures how often the president won in recorded votes in Congress on which he took a clear position, expressed as a percentage of all such votes.
- Figure 3.1 shows that President Obama's support score varied from 97% in 2009 to just 39% in 2016.
- A president's support score tends to be higher earlier in his presidency, and also when his party controls both houses of Congress – as Obama's Democrats did in 2009 and 2010.

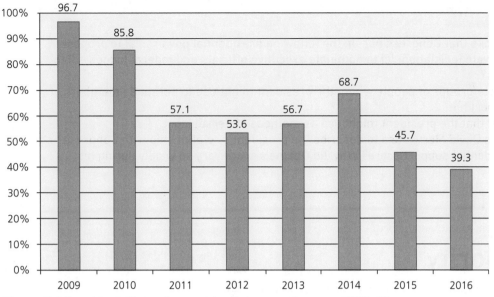

Figure 3.1 President Obama's presidential support score, 2009–16

Debate

Is the president's power still the power to persuade?

Yes	No
• President has no formal disciplinary hold over members of Congress • Party discipline in Congress, though tighter than it used to be, cannot guarantee votes for the president • President may be faced with one or both houses of Congress controlled by the other party • President is dependent upon members of Congress for legislation, confirmation of appointments, treaty ratification • President's 'direct authority' has limited use • President can offer his support for things members of Congress regard as important	• In an era of partisanship, few (if any) members of Congress from the opposition party are open to presidential persuasion, especially on big-ticket items • Partisanship also makes persuasion a less useful tool for the president trying to persuade voters to support him and then pressurise recalcitrant members of Congress to do likewise • Presidents nowadays tend to have low approval ratings (and high disapproval ratings) and therefore their persuasion is much less effective • Second-term presidents have often found their persuasive power to be very limited

---

Some quotations to use in your essays about the relations between the president and Congress include:
● The president and Congress are part of a system of 'separated institutions, sharing powers' (Richard Neustadt).
● The president and Congress are like 'two halves of a bank note, each useless without the other' (S.E. Finer).
● 'The president's power is the power to persuade' (Richard Neustadt).
● The president needs to act as 'bargainer-in-chief' (David Mervin).

TESTED

Now test yourself

22 What are the checks that Congress has on the following presidential powers: (a) to propose legislation; (b) to veto legislation; (c) to nominate executive officials and federal judges; (d) to negotiate treaties?

23 Name three people/groups of people whom the president might use to persuade members of Congress to support him.

24 Give three 'perks' that the president might use as methods of persuasion.

25 What phrase does David Mervin use to describe the president's relationship with Congress?

26 What is the presidential support score? Why did Obama's score vary so widely during his presidency?

Answers on p. 111

Direct authority

Frustrated by the checks imposed upon them as well as by the partisan gridlock in Washington, presidents have made increasing use of what is called direct authority – actions they can take which do not require congressional approval and yet can achieve some of their policy goals.

You need to be familiar with four types of direct authority.

Executive orders

REVISED

- An **executive order** is easy for a president to issue, but equally easy for a subsequent president to rescind.
- Obama made increasing use of them after the Democrats lost control of Congress.
- Trump made significant use of them during his first few months, also facing an uncooperative Congress.

> **Executive order**: An official document issued by the executive branch with the effect of law, through which the president directs federal officials to take certain actions.

Signing statements

REVISED

- George W. Bush increasingly used **signing statements** to challenge the constitutionality of some part of a bill he was signing.
- Critics claim they are an abuse of presidential power over legislation.
- Supporters see them as a way of the president getting his way over legislation even when Congress is uncooperative.

> **Signing statement**: A statement issued by the president on signing a bill which may challenge specific provisions of the bill on constitutional or other grounds.

Recess appointments

REVISED

- A **recess appointment** is another way of the president getting his way against an uncooperative Congress – this time gridlock in the Senate over confirmation of appointments.
- Bill Clinton and George W. Bush increasingly used them.
- Barack Obama lost a Supreme Court decision about them in 2014, which resulted in their curtailment.

> **Recess appointment**: A temporary appointment of a federal official made by the president to fill a vacancy while the Senate is in recess.

Executive agreements

- The president uses **executive agreements** to circumvent the Senate's power to ratify treaties.
- Hence there is strong opposition to them from Congress.

> **Executive agreement**: An agreement reached between the president and a foreign nation on matters that do not require a formal treaty.

Now test yourself

TESTED

27 What is an executive order?
28 Why do presidents tend to use them?
29 What is a signing statement?
30 What are their pros and cons?
31 What is a recess appointment?
32 Why have presidents used them?

Answers on p. 111

Theories of presidential power

Three theories of presidential power are explained in Table 3.4.

Table 3.4 Theories of presidential power

The **imperial presidency**	• Term first used by Arthur Schlesinger (1973) • Associated most with President Nixon (1969–74) • Characterised by abuse of power, secrecy (especially within the White House) and illegality
The **imperilled presidency**	• Term first used by Gerald Ford (1980) • Associated most with presidents Ford (1974–77) and Carter (1977–81) • Characterised by congressional reassertiveness and presidential weakness
The post-imperial presidency	• Term first used in 1980 • Often used to refer to presidents from Reagan to Trump • Characterised by presidential reassertiveness but power that is often limited by a new era of hyper-partisanship

> **Exam tip**
>
> When discussing presidential 'power', you need to be clear about the difference between 'powers' (the tasks of the office) that are the same for each president and 'power' (the ability to get things done) that varies between presidents and even within a presidency.

> **Imperial presidency**: A presidency characterised by the misuse of presidential powers, especially excessive secrecy – particularly in foreign policy – and high-handedness in dealing with Congress.
>
> **Imperilled presidency**: A term coined by President Gerald Ford to refer to a presidency characterised by ineffectiveness and weakness, resulting from congressional over-assertiveness.

Now test yourself

TESTED

33 Give a definition of the imperial presidency. With which president was it particularly associated?
34 Give a definition of the imperilled presidency. With which two presidents was it particularly associated?
35 What is the main characteristic of the post-imperial presidency?

Answers on p. 111

The president and foreign policy

The Constitution gives the president certain powers in foreign policy:
- to act as commander-in-chief of the armed forces
- to negotiate treaties with foreign powers
- to make certain appointments, e.g. Secretary of State, Secretary of Defense, Director of the CIA, ambassadors.

But the Constitution also gives Congress certain powers in foreign policy:
- to declare war (but not used since 1941)
- control of the budget (including military spending)
- to ratify treaties (Senate only)
- to confirm appointments (Senate only)
- to investigate (through such committees as the Senate Foreign Relations Committee, the House Armed Services Committee).

The control of foreign policy is therefore often seen as a struggle between the president and Congress.

> **Typical mistake**
>
> There are two common mistakes regarding Congress's power to declare war: to state that a super-majority is required (when it's only a simple majority); to state that only the Senate has the power (when it's both houses). Always mention that the power was last used in 1941.

> **Debate**
>
> **Does the president control foreign policy?**
>
> | Yes, because: | No, because: |
> | --- | --- |
> | <ul><li>he is commander-in-chief</li><li>he has the power to negotiate treaties</li><li>he has the power to make appointments</li><li>he can set the tone of foreign policy</li><li>he has access to the nuclear 'button' ('the football')</li><li>he 'has the facts' in a crisis</li></ul> | <ul><li>Congress controls the purse strings</li><li>only Congress can declare war (though this is largely redundant now)</li><li>the Senate has ratification power for treaties</li><li>the Senate has confirmation power of appointments</li><li>it has the power of investigation</li></ul> |

Now test yourself

TESTED ☐

36 Name the three powers related to foreign policy that the Constitution gives to the president.
37 Name three powers related to foreign policy that the Constitution gives to Congress.

Answers on pp. 111–12

Limits on presidential power

The president faces numerous checks on his power – from Congress, from the Supreme Court and from other sources, too (see Table 3.5).

Table 3.5 Checks on the president's power

Source	Checks
Congress	• Amend, delay, reject the president's legislative proposals and budgetary requests • Override the president's veto • Refuse to ratify treaties (Senate) • Refuse to confirm appointments (Senate) • Investigate the president's actions and policies • Impeach, try and remove the president from office
Supreme Court	• Declare the president's actions to be unconstitutional
Pressure groups	• Mobilise public opinion against the president's policy proposals
Public opinion	• Low approval ratings give the president less political clout
Voters	• In special and midterm elections, as well as in re-election bid
Federal bureaucracy	• Federal departments/agencies may frustrate the president's wishes
State governments	• President is often reliant upon state governments to enact his policies

So what factors can affect presidential success? See Table 3.6.

Table 3.6 Factors affecting presidential success

Electoral mandate	• Percentage of popular vote won in last election • Difference between Reagan winning 59% (1984) and Trump winning 46% (2016) • Bush (2000) and Trump (2016) both lost the popular vote
Public approval	• The higher the president's public approval rating, the more political clout he is likely to have • Difference between George W. Bush (62% approval average in first year) and Donald Trump (38% approval average in first year)
First/second term	• President likely to be more successful in first two years of first term than in last two years of second term
Unified/divided government	• Likely to be more successful if his party controls both houses of Congress (though not Clinton in 1993, or Trump in 2017)
Crises	• In a crisis, the nation tends to 'rally round the flag' and look to the president for leadership • Though if the president is seen to mishandle the crisis, it can have the opposite effect

Now test yourself

TESTED ☐

38 Name three checks that Congress has on presidential power.
39 What check does the Supreme Court have on presidential power?
40 Name three other groups/institutions that can check presidential power.
41 Name three factors that can affect presidential success.
42 What effect can crises have on presidential success?

Answers on p. 112

Comparing the president with the UK prime minister

Structural differences

There are important structural differences which one must always keep in mind whenever comparing or contrasting these two offices (see Table 3.7).

Table 3.7 Structural differences between the offices of the US president and the UK prime minister

US president	UK prime minister
The presidency is a product of revolution – the War of Independence (1776–83)	The office of the UK prime minister is a product of evolution over centuries
The president is elected as president by the people (through the Electoral College)	The prime minister is elected as party leader by the party
The position is entirely separate from the legislature	The prime minister is part of the legislature
It is limited to two terms	There are no term limits
The president is aided by an advisory cabinet	The cabinet is more than just an advisory body
He may be removed only by impeachment	The prime minister may be removed by a leadership vote in the party or as a consequence of losing a vote of confidence in the House of Commons

Comparing roles and powers

Being part of a singular executive, the US president has more in the way of roles and powers than does the UK prime minister, who is part of a plural executive working within a doctrine of collective responsibility (see Table 3.8). These significant differences in their roles and powers can largely be attributed to the structural differences mentioned in Table 3.7.

Table 3.8 Roles and powers compared

US president	UK prime minister
Fulfils roles of both head of state and chief executive	Fulfils only chief executive role (the monarch is head of state)
Has formal input only at the start and finish of the legislative process: initiating and signing/vetoing powers	Draws up government's legislative programme with the cabinet; has no veto power
Appoints cabinet, subject to Senate confirmation	Appoints cabinet (no confirmation required)
Commander-in-chief of the Armed Forces, but only Congress can declare war (though it has not done so since 1941)	Can use the royal prerogative to declare war and deploy troops abroad, but recently this has been subject to parliamentary approval
Has an elected vice president who automatically succeeds if the president dies, resigns or is removed from office	May appoint an unofficial deputy prime minister
Has (large) Executive Office of the President	Has (small) Number 10 staff and Cabinet Office
Has a variety of powers to pursue policy unilaterally: executive orders, signing statements, executive agreements	More likely to pursue policy collectively, through either the full cabinet or cabinet committees

→

US president	UK prime minister
Submits annual budget to Congress, which is then subject to months of negotiation and numerous changes	Submits annual budget to Parliament, which is debated but usually passed without any significant amendment
Appoints all federal judges	Does not appoint judges (this is done by the Judicial Appointments Commission)
Has power of pardon	Has no pardon power (only the monarch can grant a pardon)

Comparing relations with the legislature

REVISED

When comparing the president and the UK prime minister in their relations with their respective legislatures (see Table 3.9), remember that:

- whereas the president is entirely separate from Congress, the UK prime minister is not only a member of the House of Commons but also the leader of the largest party in that chamber and, as such, virtually controls its business and legislative outcomes
- whereas the president cannot be questioned by members of Congress – although members of his administration can be called before committees – the UK prime minister and their ministerial team are under constant scrutiny by Parliament.

Table 3.9 Relations with the legislature compared

US president's relations with Congress	UK prime minister's relations with Parliament
Not a serving member of Congress; must resign if serving when elected (e.g. Obama)	Serving member of Parliament
No executive branch members permitted to be serving members of Congress	Cabinet and government ministers are serving members of Parliament
Not subject to personal questioning by members of Congress	Weekly Prime Minister's Question Time (when House of Commons is sitting)
Legislative agenda often introduced in annual State of the Union Address	Legislative programme introduced in annual Queen's Speech
Gets agreement in Congress mostly by persuasion and bargaining	Gets agreement in Parliament mostly by party discipline and reliance on the payroll vote
Dependent on Senate confirmation for numerous appointments	Makes numerous appointments without the need for consent by Parliament
President's party may control only one chamber of Congress, or neither	Prime minister's party will control the House of Commons but may not have a majority in the House of Lords

Comparing cabinets

REVISED

It's tempting to say that the only similarity between these two cabinets is their name. Structural differences between the two governmental systems are again at the root of the significant differences (see Table 3.10).

Table 3.10 Significant differences between the US and the UK cabinets

US cabinet	UK cabinet
Serving members of the legislature barred from serving	Membership exclusive to Members of Parliament
Presidential appointments to the cabinet subject to Senate confirmation (though rarely rejected)	No formal limits on cabinet appointments
President decides frequency and regularity of meetings	Prime minister obliged to maintain frequency and regularity of meetings
Cabinet members are subordinate to the president, who is in no way 'first among equals'; cabinet does not take decisions – the president does	Cabinet is a collective decision-making body, at least in theory
Cabinet members recruited mostly for their policy specialisation; rarely moved to a different department	Cabinet members are usually policy generalists; hence cabinet reshuffles
Cabinet members are often strangers to the president (and sometimes to each other); no shadow cabinet	Cabinet is made up of long-serving parliamentary colleagues and former shadow cabinet members
Cabinet meetings are often the only time some cabinet members see the president	Prime minister sees cabinet colleagues regularly in Parliament
No doctrine of collective responsibility	Collective responsibility usually applies

Now test yourself

TESTED

43 Give four structural differences between the offices of the US president and the UK prime minister.
44 Give four ways in which these two offices are different in terms of their roles and powers.
45 What basic reason accounts for the different relations that the US president and the UK prime minister have with their respective legislatures?
46 Why does the author suggest that 'the only similarity between these two cabinets is their name'?

Answers on p. 112

Summary

You should now have an understanding of:
- the powers of the president
- the vice president
- the president's cabinet
- the Executive Office of the President
- the president's relations with Congress
- the president's use of direct authority
- theories of presidential power
- the role of the president in foreign policy
- limitations on presidential power
- factors that affect presidential success
- the similarities and differences between the US president and the UK prime minister

Exam practice

Section A (comparative)

1 Examine the ways in which the roles and powers of the US president and the UK prime minister are different.   [12]
2 Examine the differences in the relationship that the US president and the UK prime minister have with their respective legislatures.   [12]

Section B (comparative)

In your answer you must consider the relevance of at least one comparative theory.

1 Analyse the different ways in which the US president and the UK prime minister appoint their cabinets.   [12]
2 Analyse the different ways in which the US president and the UK prime minister are held accountable by their respective legislatures.   [12]

Section C (USA)

In your answer you must consider the stated view and the alternative to this view in a balanced way.

1 Evaluate the extent to which the president is subject to effective checks.   [30]
2 Evaluate the extent to which the president's cabinet plays a significant role within the executive branch.   [30]

Answers and quick quiz online

ONLINE

4 The Supreme Court

The Supreme Court sits atop the federal judiciary.

Below are the US Courts of Appeal (also known as Circuit Courts) and the US District Courts (also known as trial courts).

Membership of the Supreme Court

- The Court consists of nine justices (one chief justice and eight associate justices).
- These are nominated by the president.
- Their appointment needs to be confirmed by a simple majority of the Senate.
- They are appointed for life, unless impeached, found guilty and removed from office.
- The only other ways for a justice to leave the Court are by voluntary resignation (retirement), removal through impeachment, or death.
- Anthony Kennedy, appointed by Ronald Reagan in 1987, served for more than 30 years on the bench before his recent retirement.
- Chief justice at the time of writing is John Roberts (appointed by George W. Bush in 2005).
- Newest member at the time of writing is Neil Gorsuch (appointed by Donald Trump in 2017).

Now test yourself

TESTED

1 How many justices make up the Supreme Court?
2 Who nominates them?
3 How are they confirmed?
4 How long do they serve?
5 What are the only ways justices leave the Court?

Answers on p. 112

Strict constructionist: A Supreme Court justice who interprets the Constitution strictly or literally and tends to stress the retention of power by individual states.

Originalist: A Supreme Court justice who interprets the Constitution in line with the meaning or intent of the framers at the time of enactment.

Judicial philosophy

There are two main strands of judicial philosophy with which you need to be familiar, shown in Table 4.1. Examples are given in Table 4.2.

Table 4.1 The two main strands of judicial philosophy

Strict constructionists/ originalists	<ul><li>tend to interpret the Constitution in a strict, literal fashion</li><li>tend to favour state government rights over federal government power</li><li>tend to lead to an outcome that is often seen as being 'conservative'</li><li>try to interpret the Constitution in line with its original meaning and intent (hence **originalists**)</li><li>tend to be appointed by Republican presidents:
	  – e.g. John Roberts (strict constructionist)
	  – e.g. Antonin Scalia (1986–2016) (originalist)</li></ul>

Loose constructionists/ living Constitution	• tend to interpret the Constitution in a loose fashion • tend to favour federal government power over state government rights • read elements into the document that they think the framers would have approved of • see the Constitution as a living, dynamic document, which should be adapted to take account of the views of contemporary society (hence **living Constitution**) • tend to lead to an outcome that is often seen as being 'liberal' • tend to be appointed by Democratic presidents – e.g. Sonia Sotomayor, Elena Kagan

Table 4.2 The Supreme Court, 2019, by judicial philosophy

Loose constructionists	Strict constructionists
Ruth Bader Ginsburg (Clinton)	John Roberts (George W. Bush)
Stephen Breyer (Clinton)	Clarence Thomas (George H.W. Bush)
Sonia Sotomayor (Obama)	Samuel Alito (George W. Bush)
Elena Kagan (Obama)	Neil Gorsuch (Trump)

Sometimes a justice can be described as a '**swing justice**'. That was the role that Justice Anthony Kennedy played, especially between 2005 and his retirement in 2018.

Now test yourself

TESTED ☐

6 What is the difference between strict and loose constructionists?
7 Give an example of each from the current Court.
8 How would you classify justice former Anthony Kennedy?
9 What does the term 'originalist' mean?
10 If a justice believes in a 'living Constitution', what does that mean?

Answers on p. 112

Loose constructionist: A Supreme Court justice who interprets the Constitution less literally and tends to stress the broad grants of power to the federal government.

Living Constitution: The Constitution considered as a dynamic, living document, interpretation of which should take account of the views of contemporary society.

Swing justice: The pivotal justice in an otherwise evenly balanced Court, who will often be in a position of casting the deciding vote.

The appointment and confirmation process

The appointment of Supreme Court justices is a five-stage process:
1 A vacancy occurs.
2 The president instigates a search for possible nominees and interviews shortlisted candidates.
3 The president announces his nominee.
4 The Senate Judiciary Committee holds confirmation hearings on the nominee and makes a recommendatory vote.
5 The nomination is debated and voted on in the full Senate. A simple majority vote is required for confirmation.

See Table 4.3 for an example.

Exam tip

Strict construction and loose construction are technical, legal terms. Think of the word 'construction' as meaning 'interpretation'.

Table 4.3 Timeline of Supreme Court nomination, 2016–17

13 February **2016**	Associate Justice Antonin Scalia dies
16 March	President Obama nominates Judge Merrick Garland to fill vacancy, but the Republican-controlled Senate takes no action and the nomination expires
31 January, **2017**	President Trump nominates Judge Neil Gorsuch to fill vacancy
20 March	Senate Judiciary Committee begins hearings on Gorsuch nomination
3 April	Senate Judiciary Committee votes 11–9 in favour of recommending Gorsuch's confirmation
7 April	Senate votes 54–45 to confirm Gorsuch to the Supreme Court
10 April	Neil Gorsuch sworn in as Associate Justice of the Supreme Court

When appointing a new Supreme Court justice, the president is seeking to choose someone who:

- shares a similar judicial philosophy to himself
- is quite young – meaning they are likely to remain on the Court for longer
- is acceptable to a majority of the Senate (especially important if the president's party is in the minority)
- does not have a controversial background – from either a judicial or a personal point of view
- is going to be highly rated professionally (by the American Bar Association)
- has relevant experience.

> **Typical mistake**
>
> Notice that the vote in the Senate Judiciary Committee is only a recommendatory vote. The final decision is made by the full Senate – even if the nominee were to lose the committee vote.

The confirmation process has changed over recent years in that:

- Supreme Court nominees used to be approved mostly by overwhelming, bipartisan votes (e.g. Anthony Kennedy, 97–0 in 1988).
- But nowadays, although rejections are still rare, confirmation votes are much more likely to be along party lines, with pretty much all the senators from the president's party voting 'yes' and those from the other party voting 'no' (e.g. Neil Gorsuch, 54–45 in 2017 – with 51 Republicans plus 3 Democrats voting 'yes', 45 Democrats voting 'no').

> **Typical mistake**
>
> Never refer to nominees or justices as being 'Democrats' or 'Republicans'.

There are some significant criticisms of the appointment and confirmation process:

1 Presidents have tended to politicise the nominations by attempting to choose justices who share their political views and judicial philosophy (e.g. Obama with Kagan; Trump with Gorsuch).
2 The Senate has tended to politicise the confirmation process by focusing more on hot-button issues (e.g. women's rights) than on qualifications.
3 Members of the Senate Judiciary Committee from the president's party tend to ask soft questions of the nominee.
4 Members of the Senate Judiciary Committee from the opposition party attempt, through their questions, to attack or embarrass the nominee rather than to elicit relevant information.
5 Justices are now frequently confirmed on party-line votes (e.g. Gorsuch).
6 The media conduct a 'feeding frenzy' often connected with matters of trivia.

It is often said that these are the most important nominations a president makes because:

- they occur infrequently
- they are for life
- just one new appointee to a nine-member body can significantly change its philosophical balance

- the Supreme Court has the power of judicial review
- their decisions will profoundly affect the lives of ordinary Americans for generations to come.

Now test yourself

TESTED ☐

11 What are the five stages of the appointment and confirmation process?
12 What has changed in the way the Senate now votes on Supreme Court nominees?
13 Identify three significant criticisms of the appointment and confirmation process.
14 Give three reasons why these nominations are said to be the most important a president makes.

Answers on pp. 112–13

The power of judicial review

- The power of **judicial review** is not mentioned in the Constitution.
- It was 'found' by the Court in *Marbury v Madison* (1803) – regarding a federal law.
- It was used again in *Fletcher v Peck* (1810) – regarding a state law.
- It has been used since then in a host of cases to guarantee fundamental **civil rights** and **liberties**.
- Hence the Court's political importance because it rules on key political issues such as the rights of racial minorities, capital punishment, gun control and freedom of speech.
- This turns the Court into a quasi-legislative body – because the effects of its decisions have almost the effect of a law having been passed by Congress.
- For example, *Roe v Wade* (1973) had the effect comparable to an abortion rights law having been passed by Congress.
- It turns the Court into a 'third house of the legislative', a 'political' institution.

Now test yourself

TESTED ☐

15 What is the power of judicial review?
16 How did it come about?
17 What does it mean to say that this power turns the Court into a 'quasi-legislative body'?

Answers on p. 113

Judicial activism and judicial restraint

In a democracy, the people rule themselves through elected, accountable officials. But what if the courts – unelected and largely unaccountable – overturn the actions of these directly elected officials?

- Such behaviour by the courts is often referred to as **judicial activism**.
- If the courts tend to defer to the actions and decisions of elected officials – Congress and the president – this is referred to as **judicial restraint**.

> **Judicial review**: The power of the Supreme Court to declare Acts of Congress, actions of the executive, or Acts or actions of state governments unconstitutional.

> **Civil rights**: Positive acts of government designed to protect people against arbitrary or discriminatory treatment by government or individuals.

> **Civil liberties**: Those liberties, mostly spelt out in the Constitution, that guarantee the protection of people, expression and property from arbitrary interference by government.

> **Judicial activism**: An approach to judicial decision making that holds that judges should use their position to promote desirable social ends, even if that means overturning the decisions of elected officials.

> **Judicial restraint**: An approach to judicial decision making that holds that judges should defer to the legislative and executive branches, and to precedent established in previous Court decisions.

Judicial activism

- An activist Court is one that sees itself as leading the way in the reform of American society.
- It sees itself as an equal partner with the legislative and executive branches in shaping society and acting as a safeguard of civil rights and liberties.
- It is not inclined to be deferential to Congress or to the president.
- It often uses its power of judicial review to strike down Acts or actions of elected officials.
- But the term can be used with overtones of disapproval by critics of such a court.
- In such cases, judicial activism may be labelled as 'legislating from the bench' by an 'imperial judiciary'.

> **Typical mistake**
>
> When discussing particular decisions of the Court, do so from an academic and philosophical perspective, not from a personal perspective. The examiner does not want to know whether you personally are in favour of or opposed to, for example, a woman's right

Examples of recent cases in which the Supreme Court has clearly taken the lead in shaping American society in terms of its rights and liberties are:
- *Roe v Wade* (1973) – guaranteed a woman's right to choose an abortion.
- *District of Columbia v Heller* (2008) – guaranteed individual gun ownership rights.
- *Obergefell v Hodges* (2015) – guaranteed rights to same-sex marriage.

Judicial activism could also be seen in the case of *Bush v Gore* (2000), which effectively awarded the presidency to George W. Bush after a disputed vote count in Florida.

Judicial restraint

- A restrained Court is one that is more inclined to accept the actions and decisions of elected officials.
- It sees Congress and the president – not itself – as the shapers of American society.
- Where possible, it tends to defer to the precedent laid down in previous Court decisions (**stare decisis**).
- A more accurate term may be 'judicial deference'.

> **Stare decisis**: A legal principle that judges should look to past precedents as a guide wherever possible (literally, 'let the decision stand').

Now test yourself

18 What is meant by judicial activism?
19 Give two recent examples of the Court's decision reshaping American society.
20 What is meant by judicial restraint?
21 What does the term *stare decisis* mean?

Answers on p. 113

The Supreme Court and the Bill of Rights

The Constitution's framers wanted to guarantee fundamental rights and liberties of American citizens (see Chapter 1).

To do so, they added the Bill of Rights – the first ten amendments – to the Constitution.

> **Exam tip**
>
> In your exam answers, don't spend time telling the narrative of cases, except in the briefest outline. We don't need to know who the people are involved in each case. Get to the significance of the case – tell the examiner what the case illustrates.

First Amendment: freedom of religion

Zelman v Simmons-Harris (2002): the Court upheld an Ohio state programme giving financial aid to parents, allowing them, if they so chose, to send their children to a religious or private school.
- *Significance*: state government money could be finding its way to a religious, private school.

Town of Greece v Galloway (2014): the Court allowed legislative bodies (such as town councils) to begin their meetings with prayer.
- *Significance*: strengthened individuals' rights to practise their religion in public, even in state-constituted and state-funded bodies.

Burwell v Hobby Lobby Stores Inc (2010): the Court overturned the requirement under the Affordable Care Act (2010) (otherwise known as Obamacare) that family-owned firms had to pay for health insurance coverage for contraception as this violated the religious beliefs of some Christian-run companies.
- *Significance*: strengthened individual rights of Christian business executives to run their companies along lines that agreed with their religious beliefs.

> **Typical mistake**
>
> Don't use overly dated examples, except maybe when they are really landmark decisions, like *Roe v Wade*. But even then, always give a more recent abortion rights decision as well to show that your knowledge is up to date.

First Amendment: freedom of speech

McConnell v Federal Election Commission (2004): upheld federal law (Bipartisan Campaign Reform Act) banning soft money in election campaigns, stating that this ban did not violate freedom of speech.
- *Significance*: limiting campaign finance is not incompatible with the freedom of speech provision of the Constitution.

Citizens United v FEC (2010): ruled that when it comes to rights of political speech, business corporations and labour unions have the same rights as individuals.
- *Significance*: opened the door to unlimited spending by corporations in election campaigns, mostly funnelled through political action committees (PACs).

McCutcheon v FEC (2014): struck down a 1970s' limit on totals that wealthy individuals can contribute to candidates and PACs.
- *Significance*: reaffirmed giving of money to candidates and PACs as a fundamental right.

Second Amendment: gun control

District of Columbia v Heller (2008): guaranteed individual gun ownership rights.

McDonald v City of Chicago (2010): extended the rights announced in *Heller* to state and local governments.
- *Significance*: never before had the courts ruled this interpretation of the Second Amendment.

Eighth Amendment: death penalty

Roper v Simmons (2005): declared it to be unconstitutional to sentence anyone to death for a crime they committed when under the age of 18.

Glossip v Gross (2015): declared that lethal injection did not infringe the Eighth Amendment's ban on 'cruel punishments'.

- *Significance*: the Court was clearly seen as telling us what 18th-century words mean in 21st-century America.

> **Exam tip**
>
> **How to use these cases in your exam answers**
>
> You can use these decisions as examples of the Supreme Court:
> - guaranteeing and guarding the rights and liberties granted in the Bill of Rights (e.g. freedom of speech, freedom from cruel punishments)
> - interpreting words written in the 18th century and saying what they mean today (e.g. 'freedom of speech', 'freedom of religion', 'right to keep and bear arms', freedom from 'cruel and unusual punishments')
> - becoming a political institution, in that it is making decisions on policy that are fought over in election campaigns (e.g. death penalty, gun control)
> - giving the Court a quasi-legislative function (as it were, rewriting or deleting parts of the Bipartisan Campaign Reform Act and the Affordable Care Act).

Now test yourself

TESTED

22 Give two examples of recent Supreme Court decisions relating to freedom of religion and explain the significance of each.
23 Give two examples of recent Supreme Court decisions relating to freedom of speech and explain the significance of each.
24 What was the significance of recent Supreme Court decisions on gun control?
25 What was the significance of recent Supreme Court decisions on the death penalty?

Answers on pp. 113–14

The Supreme Court and public policy

As well as interpreting the Bill of Rights, the Supreme Court decides cases affecting matters of public policy that are at the forefront of American political debate.

Abortion

REVISED

Roe v Wade (1973): ruled that the state law of Texas forbidding abortion was unConstitutional.
- *Significance*: guaranteed a woman's right to choose an abortion as a constitutionally protected right.

Gonzales v Carhart (2007): upheld the Partial Birth Abortion Act (2003), which banned late-term abortions.
- *Significance*: established that a woman's right to choose an abortion could be legally limited.

Whole Woman's Health v Hellerstedt (2016): struck down as unconstitutional two parts of a Texas state law concerning abortion provision.

- *Significance*: not all limits on a woman's right to choose would be regarded as constitutionally permissible.

Marriage equality

REVISED

United States v Windsor (2013): declared the Defense of Marriage Act (1996) to be unconstitutional and that it is unconstitutional to treat same-sex married couples differently from other married couples in terms of federal benefits.

Obergefell v Hodges (2015): declared that state bans on same-sex marriage were unconstitutional.

- *Significance*: shows how the Court can reshape American society on a contemporary and contentious issue.

Exam tip

How to use these cases in your exam answers

You can use these decisions as examples of the Supreme Court:

- guaranteeing and guarding the rights and liberties granted in the Constitution (e.g. rights of liberty and the equal protection of the laws – Fourteenth Amendment)
- interpreting what words written in 1868 (Fourteenth Amendment) mean in modern-day America
- becoming a political institution, in that it is making decisions on policy that are fought over in election campaigns (e.g. abortion and gay rights)
- giving the Court a quasi-legislative function (declaring a 1996 law unconstitutional).

Debate

Is the Supreme Court a political institution?

Yes	No
<ul><li>Appointed by a politician (the president)</li><li>Confirmed by politicians (the Senate)</li><li>Makes decisions on issues that feature in elections (e.g. abortion, gun control, marriage equality) and over which the two main parties disagree</li><li>Some of its decisions have a quasi-legislative effect: it is as if a new law has been passed, and passing laws is what politicians do</li><li>Some have described the Court as 'a third house of the legislature'</li></ul>	<ul><li>Its members are judges, not politicians</li><li>The Court is independent – not subject to political pressure</li><li>Justices do not involve themselves in party politics, elections, campaigning, endorsing candidates</li><li>There is no such thing as a Democratic justice or a Republican justice</li><li>Members make decisions based on legal and constitutional argument, not political ideology</li></ul>

Now test yourself

TESTED

26 Give two examples of recent Supreme Court decisions relating to abortion and explain their significance.
27 Give two examples of recent Supreme Court decisions relating to marriage equality and explain their significance.

Answers on p. 114

The Supreme Court and federal government power

Through its power of judicial review, the Supreme Court also has the power to rule on the actions of both Congress and the president and to rule when, in their judgement, they exceed their constitutional powers.

National Federation of Independent Business v Sebelius (2012): upheld most of the provisions of the Affordable Care Act (2010) but ruled that the Act's requirement that every American had to either get health insurance or pay a penalty could not be justified by Congress's powers under the Commerce Clause, only by its power to collect taxes.

National Labor Relations Board v Noel Canning (2014): declared President Obama's 'recess appointments' to the NLRB in 2012 to be unconstitutional as the Senate was not technically in recess.

- *Significance*: the Court shows its power to say what Congress and the president can and cannot do according to its interpretation of their respective constitutional powers.

> **Exam tip**
>
> **How to use these cases in your exam answers**
> You can use these decisions as examples of the Supreme Court:
> - interpreting the words of the Constitution, written centuries ago, and saying what they mean in 21st-century America
> - acting as an umpire over the checks and balances of the Constitution
> - preventing either branch of government from exceeding its powers.

Now test yourself   TESTED

28 Give an example of a recent Supreme Court decision on the powers of Congress.
29 Give an example of a recent Supreme Court decision on the powers of the president.

Answers on p. 114

Checks on the power of the Supreme Court

The Supreme Court, like the other two branches of the federal government, is subject to various checks and balances. These include the following.

Checks by Congress   REVISED

- The Senate has the power to confirm or reject appointments.
- Congress fixes the numerical size of the Court.
- Congress has the power of impeachment – even the threat of impeachment is a check.
- Congress can initiate constitutional amendments that would have the effect of overturning the Court's decision.

Checks by the president

- The president has the power to nominate justices.
- He can decide whether to throw his political weight behind a decision of the Court, thereby either enhancing or decreasing the Court's perceived legitimacy.

Other checks

- The Court has no power of initiation: it must wait for cases to be brought before it.
- The Court has no enforcement powers: it is dependent on the other branches of government and/or the rule of law for implementation of and obedience to Court decisions.
- Public opinion: if the Court makes decisions that are regarded as wrong by a majority of the public, the Court loses some of its legitimacy.
- The Court is checked by itself – by decisions it has already made.
- The Court is checked by the Constitution – although certain parts of the Constitution are open to the Court's interpretation, other parts are very specific.

Exam tip

These checks would form a significant part of an answer to a question about whether the Supreme Court has 'too much power'.

Debate

Does the Supreme Court have too much power?

Yes	No
• The Court gave itself the power of judicial review • It has declared more Acts of Congress unconstitutional as the decades have passed • It has made decisions that are out of line with the majority of public opinion • It is an unelected body • It is a largely unaccountable body • It has abused its power to bring about significant policy change (e.g. abortion, same-sex marriage) • Yes – when justices believe in a living constitution	• It is checked by Congress, which may initiate constitutional amendments effectively overriding Court decisions • Congress has the power of impeachment • It has no initiative power: must wait for cases to come before it • It is dependent upon the rule of law and other branches of government to enforce its decisions • Public opinion is a restraining force on the Court's power • It is checked by the words of the Constitution: where it is precise and not open to interpretation by the Court

Now test yourself

30 Give two examples of the way Congress can check the Supreme Court.
31 Give two examples of the way the president can check the Supreme Court.
32 Give two other factors that can act as checks on the Supreme Court.

Answers on p. 114

Comparing the US and UK Supreme Courts

Origins

The origins of the two Supreme Courts could hardly be more different:

- The US Supreme Court:
  - created by the founding fathers in 1787
  - written into the Constitution (Article III)
  - the only federal court created at that time
  - shared building space with Congress until 1935
  - then moved to purpose-built building on Capitol Hill.
- The UK Supreme Court:
  - created by Act of Parliament
  - came into existence in October 2009
  - was the last part of the UK court structure to be created
  - replaced the Appellate Committee of the House of Lords as the nation's highest court
  - given converted building space (old Middlesex Guildhall) in Parliament Square.

These differences reflect the structural and cultural differences between the USA and the UK:

- Structural: whereas the USA is based on a system of 'separated institutions, sharing powers' and checks and balances, the UK is based on a system of fused powers in which, until very recently, the three branches of government overlapped.
- Cultural: whereas the USA came into existence at one given moment – with the writing of the federal Constitution in 1787 – the UK has evolved gradually over centuries without a codified constitution.

Appointments, membership and tenure

These structural and cultural differences also account for significant differences in the appointments, membership and tenure of the two Supreme Courts (see Table 4.4).

Table 4.4 US and UK Supreme Courts: structural and cultural differences

	US Supreme Court	UK Supreme Court
Appointments made by	• Nominated by the president • Require confirmation by the Senate	• Nominated by the Judicial Appointments Commission • No confirmation required
Membership	• Currently 9 members • Number fixed by Congress • Currently includes 3 women • Presided over by the Chief Justice of the United States • All justices hear all cases (unless recused)	• 12 members • Currently includes 2 women • Presided over by the President of the Supreme Court • Between 5 and 11 justices hear cases
Tenure	• Life tenure • Subject to impeachment, trial and removal by Congress	• Must retire at 70 if appointed to a judicial office after 1995; otherwise 75 • Subject to removal by the monarch following an address by both houses of Parliament

Powers and roles

The most significant power of the US Supreme Court is its power of judicial review (see Table 4.5).

The UK Supreme Court also has the power of judicial review, but the terms do not mean the same thing in the two systems (see Table 4.6).

Table 4.5 Judicial review in the US and UK Supreme Courts

US Supreme Court	UK Supreme Court
• Not explicitly granted in the Constitution • 'Found' by the Court in *Marbury v Madison* (1803) – i.e. the Court gave itself the power • Judicial review is the power to declare Acts (of the legislature) or actions (of the executive) of the federal or state governments unConstitutional • Resulted in greatly enhanced political importance for the Court	• Judicial review does not allow the Court to declare Acts of Parliament unconstitutional • Because the Court operates in a system ruled by the doctrine of parliamentary sovereignty • But it can declare actions of ministers to be *ultra vires* – that is, beyond the powers granted by Parliament • This has given the Court increasing importance since its creation in 2009

Ultra vires: Latin phrase (literally, 'beyond the powers') used to describe an action that is beyond one's legal power or authority.

Table 4.6 The powers and roles of the US and UK Supreme Courts

US Supreme Court	UK Supreme Court
• Final court of appeal for federal cases • Also hears cases on appeal from state supreme courts • Rules on the constitutionality of federal and state laws (judicial review) • Rules on the constitutionality of actions of the federal and state executives (judicial review) • Rules on the meaning of the Constitution • Acts as interpreter and guardian of civil rights and liberties	• Final court of appeal for all UK civil cases and for criminal cases in England, Wales and Northern Ireland • Cannot overrule or strike down the laws passed by the UK Parliament – though can interpret the laws passed by Parliament • Rules on whether or not actions taken by ministers are *ultra vires*

Judicial independence

Judicial independence is a vital ingredient of a democracy to ensure that judges are free from external pressures.

Such pressure might come from:
- the executive
- the legislature
- pressure groups
- the media
- other judges, especially senior judges.

Judicial independence is protected by the fact that:
- judges have immunity from prosecution for any acts they carry out as judges
- they have immunity from lawsuits of defamation for what they say while hearing cases
- judges' salaries cannot be reduced.

See Table 4.7.

Table 4.7 Judicial independence in the USA and the UK

In the USA	In the UK
<ul><li>Judicial independence enhanced by life tenure</li><li>Strengthened when justices decide a case in a way that is clearly not in line with the views of the president who appointed them, e.g. Clinton appointees who found against Clinton in *Clinton v Jones* (1997)</li><li>But seemingly undermined when judges appear to make politicised judgments, e.g. *Bush v Gore* (2000)</li><li>Under pressure when presidents make verbal attacks on the judiciary or on individual judges, e.g. Trump over court's decision on his travel ban (2017)</li></ul>	<ul><li>Judicial independence was somewhat compromised all the time the Law Lords sat in the House of Lords (were part of the legislature)</li><li>Still some ambiguities in roles of Lord Chancellor, Attorney General and Solicitor General</li><li>Under pressure recently from attacks by politicians, notably about the High Court's ruling concerning the triggering of Article 50 in the Brexit implementation</li><li>Recent media attacks on the judiciary: 'Enemies of the People'</li></ul>

Now test yourself

TESTED ☐

33 Give three ways in which the US and UK Supreme Courts differ in terms of their origins.

34 Give two reasons for these differences.

35 How do the appointment processes to the US and UK Supreme Courts differ?

36 How do the two Supreme Courts differ in terms of the tenure of the judges?

37 What does the term *ultra vires* mean? Why is it important in the UK Supreme Court?

38 Name three potential sources of pressure on judicial independence.

39 Give two ways in which judicial independence is protected.

Answers on p. 114

Summary

You should now have an understanding of:
- the membership of the Supreme Court
- the philosophy of the justices
- the appointment and confirmation process
- the power of judicial review
- judicial activism and judicial restraint
- the Supreme Court and the Bill of Rights
- the Supreme Court and public policy
- the Supreme Court and federal government power
- checks on the Supreme Court
- the similarities and differences between the US and UK Supreme Courts

Exam practice

Section A (comparative)

1 Examine the differences between the US and UK Supreme Courts in terms of membership and tenure. [12]
2 Examine the role played by judicial review in the US and UK Supreme Courts. [12]

Section B (comparative)

In your answer you must consider the relevance of at least one comparative theory.
1 Analyse the differences in the origins of the US and UK Supreme Courts. [12]
2 Analyse the differences in the ways in which members of the US and UK Supreme Courts are appointed. [12]

Section C (USA)

In your answer you must consider the stated view and the alternative to this view in a balanced way.
1 Evaluate the extent to which the Supreme Court has quasi-legislative powers. [30]
2 Evaluate the extent to which the nomination and confirmation process of Supreme Court justices has been politicised. [30]

Answers and quick quiz online

ONLINE

5 Civil rights and liberties

Civil rights of racial minorities in the USA have been advanced through various political means:
- constitutional amendment, e.g. the Twenty-fourth Amendment (1964)
- legislation, e.g. Voting Rights Act (1965)
- decision of the Supreme Court, e.g. *Brown v Board of Education of Topeka* (1954)
- presidential leadership, e.g. President Eisenhower's use of federal troops in Little Rock, Arkansas (1957)
- citizen action, e.g. March for Jobs and Freedom (1963).

> **Civil rights:** Positive acts of government designed to protect persons against arbitrary or discriminatory treatment by government or individuals.

Typical mistake

Don't turn your answers into an historical summary. Yes, you need to know the roots of the civil rights movement, but only – at the most – to refer to briefly, if relevant.

Exam tip

When giving examples in your answers, always use the most up-to-date examples that are relevant.

Civil rights of other societal groups relating to, for example, gender, disability and sexual orientation have also been advanced through a similar variety of political means:
- by constitutional amendment, e.g. Nineteenth Amendment (1920) – women's right to vote
- by legislation, e.g. Americans with Disabilities Act (1990) – rights of the physically disabled
- by decision of the Supreme Court, e.g. *Obergefell v Hodges* (2015) – right to same-sex marriage.

Civil liberties in the USA (as seen in Chapter 4) have been mainly advanced and protected by the Bill of Rights (Amendments I–X of the Constitution) plus subsequent decisions of the Supreme Court.

> **Civil liberties:** Those liberties, mostly spelt out in the Constitution, that guarantee the protection of persons, expression and property from arbitrary interference by government.

Now test yourself

TESTED

1 Define the terms 'civil rights' and 'civil liberties'.
2 Name three means by which the civil rights of racial minorities have been advanced.
3 Give two examples of the ways in which the rights of other societal groups have been advanced.

Answers on pp. 114–15

Affirmative action

Affirmative action promotes equality of results rather than merely equality of opportunity (see Table 5.1).

It was meant to lead to diversity and multiculturalism in education, employment, housing, etc.

In order to achieve this, quota programmes and **busing** (in school allocation) would be necessary.

> **Affirmative action:** A programme giving members of a previously disadvantaged minority group a head start in, for example, higher education or employment.

> **Busing:** The mandated movement of school children between racially homogeneous neighbourhoods – white suburbs and black inner cities – to create racially mixed schools.

Table 5.1 Difference between equality of opportunity and equality of results

Equality of opportunity	Equality of results
● Focuses on giving the same rights and opportunities to all ● Focuses on the theory of rights and of equality rather than its outworking ● Regards affirmative action programmes as 'reverse discrimination' ● Believes all rights should be 'colour blind'	● Focuses on outcomes ● Focuses on giving advantages to previously disadvantaged groups in order to bring about equality in reality, not just in theory ● Advocates such schemes as affirmative action and **quotas**

> **Quotas**: A programme by which a certain percentage (quota) of places in, for example, higher education or employment are reserved for people from previously disadvantaged minorities.

Affirmative action and the Supreme Court

REVISED

In various cases, the Supreme Court both advanced and regulated affirmative action programmes, especially as they related to school and university admission processes (see Table 5.2).

Table 5.2 Examples of Supreme Court decisions

Supreme Court decision	Ruled that ...
Gratz v Bollinger (2003)	The University of Michigan's affirmative action-based admissions programme was unconstitutional because it was too 'mechanistic'; all minority students were automatically awarded bonus marks regardless of whether they had experienced disadvantage
Grutter v Bollinger (2003)	The University of Michigan's Law School's admissions programme was upheld because it used a more 'individualised' approach
Parents Involved v Seattle School District (2007)	It is unconstitutional to assign students to public (i.e. state-run) schools solely for the purpose of achieving racial balance
Fisher v University of Texas (2013)	The university's use of race in its admission policy must be subjected to a stricter scrutiny because it involved possible discrimination against white students
Fisher v University of Texas (2016)	(A rehearing of the 2013 case.) The university's admission programme based on affirmative action was constitutional

Pros and cons of affirmative action

REVISED

- Republicans and conservatives tend to argue against affirmative action programmes, claiming that they merely perpetuate decisions being made based on race.
- Democrats and liberals tend to argue in favour of affirmative action programmes, claiming that they have made society more diverse and given equality of results to previously disadvantaged groups.

The advantages and disadvantages are summed up in Table 5.3.

Table 5.3 Affirmative action: advantages and disadvantages

Advantages of affirmative action	Disadvantages of affirmative action
• Leads to greater levels of diversity • Rights previous wrongs – those previously disadvantaged are now advantaged • Opens up areas of education and employment that otherwise would be out of the reach of disadvantaged minorities • In education, creates a more diverse student body, thereby promoting integration and racial tolerance	• Advantage for one group leads to disadvantage for other groups – 'reverse discrimination' • Can lead to minorities being admitted to higher education courses and jobs with which they are ill-equipped to cope • Can be condescending to minorities • Perpetuates a society based on colour and race

Now test yourself

TESTED

4 What is affirmative action?
5 What is 'busing'?
6 What are 'quotas'?
7 Explain the difference between 'equality of opportunity' and 'equality of results'.
8 Give two examples of recent Supreme Court decisions regarding affirmative action.
9 Give three advantages and three disadvantages of affirmative action.

Answers on p. 115

Voting rights and minority representation

There have been significant strides in widening voting rights through:
• legislation, e.g. Voting Rights Act (1965) and the re-authorisation of key parts of this Act in 2006
• voter registration drives among black and Hispanic communities
• voter turnout drives among the same groups.

But concerns still exist:
• introduction by some states of photo ID requirement at polling stations
• removal of voting rights following criminal convictions.

Minority representation has increased steadily in recent decades:
• in Congress: black members up from 16 in 1979–80 to 49 in 2017–18; Hispanic/Latino members up from 6 in 1979–80 to 38 in 2017–18
• in presidential candidates: Barack Obama winning the Democratic nomination and the presidency (2008); three ethnic minority candidates ran for Republican nomination in 2016 – Ben Carson, Bobby Jindal, Marco Rubio
• in the president's cabinet: Barack Obama's initial cabinet (2009) was the most racially diverse to date – out of 15 heads of executive departments, 7 were from ethnic minorities; George W. Bush (2001–09) was served throughout by people of colour as secretary of state – Colin Powell followed by Condoleezza Rice.

Now test yourself

10 Give two examples of ways in which voting rights have been advanced.
11 Give an example of a concern about voting rights.
12 To what extent has minority representation increased in Congress since 1979–80?
13 Name two racial minority candidates who ran for the Republican presidential nomination in 2016.
14 How ethnically diverse was President Obama's first cabinet?

Answers on p. 115

Immigration reform

This issue has come very much to the fore during the past two decades.

It has been fuelled by concerns over illegal immigration, security fears following 9/11 and the fate of those Americans brought illegally to the United States by their parents in previous decades.

- George W. Bush tried to get immigration reform through Congress but failed.
- Barack Obama got Congress to pass the Development, Relief, and Education for Alien Minors (DREAM) Act.
- Obama also created the DACA programme (Deferred Action for Childhood Arrivals) in 2012, which allowed some individuals who entered the country as the children of illegal immigrants to have the temporary right to live, study and work in the USA.
- During the 2016 election, Donald Trump announced his intention to end the DACA programme, make the deportation of all illegal immigrants a top priority, and build a wall along the USA–Mexico border.
- In January 2018, Trump's intention to carry through on his threat to end the DACA programme was a contributory factor in a short-term partial shutdown of parts of the federal government.

> **Exam tip**
>
> Always avoid expressing your personal preferences and prejudices in your answers.

Now test yourself

15 What did President Obama manage to achieve in terms of immigration reform?
16 What is the DACA programme?
17 What measures has President Trump proposed regarding illegal immigrants?

Answers on p. 115

Comparing the protection of rights in the USA and the UK

The most significant difference is that in the USA, rights are entrenched in a codified constitution, whereas in the UK, with no codified constitution, rights are not entrenched and can be changed simply by Act of Parliament. This shows that different structures produce different outcomes.

So where do we find the rights of citizens in the USA and the UK? Consider Table 5.4.

Table 5.4 The rights of citizens in the USA and in the UK

In the USA	In the UK
<ul><li>Bill of Rights (Amendments I–X of the Constitution)</li><li>Later amendments, e.g. Fifteenth, Nineteenth, Twenty-Fourth, Twenty-Sixth</li><li>Laws passed by Congress, e.g.:<ul><li>various Civil Rights Acts</li><li>Voting Rights Act (1965)</li><li>Americans with Disabilities Act (1990)</li><li>Fair Pay Act (2009)</li></ul></li><li>Decisions of the Supreme Court, e.g.:<ul><li>*Roe v Wade* (1973)</li><li>*Obergefell v Hodges* (2015)</li></ul></li></ul>	<ul><li>Acts of Parliament, e.g. Human Rights Act (1998), which incorporated the European Convention on Human Rights into British law</li><li>Decisions of the courts that protect citizens against unlawful acts of government, e.g.:<ul><li>extent of government spying powers</li><li>length of time police can keep DNA of acquitted persons</li><li>whole-life sentences must be reviewable</li><li>employers must respect religious beliefs of employees</li></ul></li></ul>

Effectiveness of the protection of rights

REVISED

Effectiveness of the protection of rights is key to a liberal democracy. Constitutions and laws don't in themselves deliver rights.

- Some see the protection of the rights of one group leading to a threat to the rights of another group, e.g. same-sex marriage rights as opposed to the rights of groups and individuals that take an orthodox Christian view of marriage.
- This issue has led to court battles in both the USA and the UK.
- Also effective protection of rights needs to be balanced against the need for security in the light of terrorist threats.
- This is another issue that has led to much debate in both countries.
- But a combination of legislative and judicial action means that the rights of racial minorities, women and those with physical disabilities are better protected than they were half a century ago.
- Note the significant role played by pressure groups in both countries to promote the effective protection of a range of rights, e.g. ACLU, NAACP in the USA; Liberty and Stonewall in the UK.

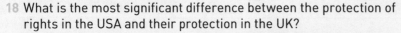

Now test yourself

TESTED

18 What is the most significant difference between the protection of rights in the USA and their protection in the UK?
19 Name three places where the rights of US citizens can be found.
20 Name two places where the rights of UK citizens can be found.
21 Give an example of where protecting the rights of two opposing groups has led to clashes in the courts in both countries.
22 What issue regarding rights has the terrorist threat in both countries raised?
23 Name two pressure groups from each country that are at the forefront of the protection of civil rights.

Answers on p. 115

Summary

You should now have an understanding of:
- civil rights and liberties
- affirmative action
- voting rights
- minority representation
- immigration reform
- the similarities and differences between the protection of rights in the USA and in the UK

Exam practice

Section A (comparative)

1 Examine the role pressure groups play in the protection of rights in the USA and the UK. [12]

Section B (comparative)

In your answer you must consider the relevance of at least one comparative theory.

1 Analyse the differences between the ways in which rights are protected in the USA and the UK. [12]

Section C (USA)

In your answer you must consider the stated view and the alternative to this view in a balanced way.

1 Evaluate the extent to which decisions of the Supreme Court have weakened affirmative action programmes in the USA. [30]

Answers and quick quiz online

ONLINE

6 Elections

Presidential elections

When presidential elections occur

Fixed-term elections are held every four years (Article II).

If the president dies in office, resigns or is removed from office by impeachment, the vice president automatically and immediately becomes president and serves out the remainder of the president's term.

Federal law fixes the election as the Tuesday after the first Monday in November (i.e. between 2 and 8 November).

Requirements for a presidential candidate

Constitutional requirements are:
- natural-born American citizen
- at least 35 years old
- resided within the USA for at least 14 years
- also, since 1951, not to have already served two terms (Twenty-second Amendment).

Other (extra-constitutional) requirements:
- political experience (though neither Eisenhower nor Trump had any)
- major party endorsement
- ability to raise large sums of money
- effective organisation
- oratorical skills; telegenic
- sound and relevant policies.

Now test yourself

1 How often do presidential elections occur?
2 What are the three constitutional requirements to be president?
3 How does the Twenty-second Amendment impact the requirements to be president?

Answers on p. 115

There are seven stages in a presidential election:
1 The **invisible primary**.
2 Primaries and caucuses.
3 Choosing vice presidential candidate(s).
4 National party conventions.
5 General election campaign.
6 Election Day.
7 Electoral College voting.

> **Invisible primary**: The period between candidates declaring an intention to run for the presidency and the first primaries and caucuses.

The invisible primary

The invisible primary period – effectively the calendar year before the election – features:

- candidate announcements
- televised party debates
- fundraising
- raising national name recognition for lesser-known candidates
- opinion polls showing who are the front-runners
- endorsements by leading party figures (e.g. members of Congress, state governors, former presidents).

Debate

Is the invisible primary important?

Yes, because...	No, because...
• the candidate leading in the polls at the end of the invisible primary is very often the one eventually chosen after the primaries • some candidates even drop out during this period (e.g. five Republicans and two Democrats in 2015) • critical for fundraising as the primaries and caucuses are packed into the early months of election year • first impressions in the televised party debates are important	• it's possible to 'win' the invisible primary but go on to lose the nomination (e.g. Democrats Howard Dean in 2003–04 and Hillary Clinton in 2007–08) • candidates who drop out don't do so just because of the invisible primary but because they are ill-qualified and/or unpopular candidates • it doesn't test campaigning skills as well as the primaries do, and especially the caucuses • the focus is mainly on performance (in the debates and polls) rather than on policies

Now test yourself

TESTED

4 What is the invisible primary?
5 When does it occur?
6 Name three important things that occur during this period.

Answers on p. 115

Primaries and caucuses

REVISED

This is the second stage of the presidential election.

- **Primaries** are held in mid- to large-population states (e.g. California, New York, North Carolina, Alabama).
- **Caucuses** are held in some small- to mid-population states, and especially in geographically large states with small populations (e.g. Iowa, Utah, Alaska, Wyoming).
- Any registered voter can participate.
- They have two main functions:
  - to show popularity for candidates among ordinary voters
  - to choose delegates to go to the national party conventions.
- State parties decide whether to hold a primary or caucuses.

Primary: A state-based election to choose a party's candidate for the presidency. It shows support for candidates among ordinary voters.

Caucuses: A state-based series of meetings to choose a party's candidate for the presidency. They usually attract unrepresentative and low turnouts.

Typical mistake

Notice the term 'caucuses' is plural – because in any given state that holds them there will be literally dozens of them all over the state. Hence we talk about 'the Iowa caucuses', not 'the Iowa caucus'.

Timing of primaries

- States decide on timing of primaries and caucuses.
- The usual window is January/February to June of election year.
- Some states schedule early contests, e.g. Iowa, New Hampshire.
- Some states deliberately coincide their contests on the same day as those of neighbouring states, creating a regional primary, e.g. **Super Tuesday**.
- Election cycles between 1984 and 2008 saw an increase in **front loading**, with more and more states pushing their dates earlier in the cycle (but 2012 and 2016 saw some slippage in this trend).

Types of primary

There are two different ways of classifying primaries. First is by who is allowed to vote in them:

- open primaries: in which any registered voter can vote in either party's primary
- closed primaries: in which only registered Democrats can vote in the Democratic primary and only registered Republicans can vote in the Republican primary
- modified primaries: like closed primaries, but also allow registered independents to vote in either party's primary.

Second, we also classify primaries by how delegates are awarded in them:

- proportional primaries: in which delegates are awarded to the candidates in proportion to the votes they get (there is normally a threshold a candidate must reach to win any delegates, usually set at 10% or 15%)
- winner-take-all primaries: in which whoever gets the most votes in the primary wins all that state's delegates (allowed only in the Republican Party).

Early primaries and caucuses

Iowa traditionally holds the first presidential caucuses:

- Often attracts very low turnout (just 2,108 voters in 2012 Republican caucuses).
- Turnout is also unrepresentative because Iowa is more than 90% white and caucuses also tend to attract the more ideological voters.
- Their record of predicting the eventual nominee is mixed (Senator Ted Cruz won the 2016 Republican caucuses).
- But they can be crucial (e.g. Hillary Clinton's defeat by Barack Obama in the 2008 Democratic caucuses).

New Hampshire traditionally holds the first presidential primary:

- Often attracts the highest turnout – 52% in 2016.
- But the state is around 94% white, so it is unrepresentative of the USA as a whole (74% white).
- It is possible to lose the New Hampshire primary but still win the party nomination, e.g. George W. Bush (Republicans 2000), Bob Dole (Republicans 1996), Bill Clinton (Democrats 1992).
- The most important thing for a candidate is to live up to or exceed expectations.
- Winning the New Hampshire primary brings a boost in opinion poll numbers, media coverage and money.

Super Tuesday: A Tuesday in February or early March when a number of states coincide their presidential primaries and caucuses to try to gain influence.

Front loading: The phenomenon by which states schedule their primaries or caucuses earlier in the nomination cycles in an attempt to increase their importance.

Typical mistake

Don't forget that any registered voter can participate in the primaries and caucuses – they are not limited to party members.

Typical mistake

Don't refer to proportional primaries as 'proportional representation'. That's something quite different.

Incumbent presidents and primaries

Incumbent presidents (e.g. George W. Bush in 2004; Barack Obama in 2012) have to compete in their party's primaries, but little or no attention is given to these primaries.

- Bush won 98% of the vote in the 2004 Republican primaries; Obama 92% of the vote in the 2012 Democratic primaries.
- But this all changes if the incumbent president faces a serious primary challenge (e.g. Jimmy Carter facing Senator Edward Kennedy in the 1980 Democratic primaries; Georg H.W. Bush facing Pat Buchanan in the 1992 Republican primaries).
- It was not coincidental that although Carter and Bush won their primaries, they both went on to lose in the general election, having been politically damaged in the primaries.
- So the key for an incumbent president is to avoid a serious primary challenge.

> **Incumbent**: A person who currently holds an office – in this case an elective office (the presidency).

Voter turnout in primaries

Voter turnout in primaries tends to be low – somewhere between 20 and 30% of eligible voters.

- Turnout varies from state to state, e.g. in 2016 it varied from 52% in the New Hampshire primary to just 5.5% in the Kansas caucuses.
- Turnout is higher in primaries than in caucuses.
- Factors that affect turnout in primaries and caucuses include:
  - demography – higher among more educated, higher-income and elderly voters
  - type of primary – open primaries tend to attract higher turnout as more people are eligible to vote in them
  - competitiveness (or otherwise) of the nomination race – turnout is higher if the nomination race is competitive; lower if it's a one-horse race
  - timing – primaries that are held after the nomination has effectively been decided attract lower turnout than those held when the race is still open.

Debate

Are primaries important?

Yes, because...	No, because...
<ul><li>the presidential candidates emerge during them</li><li>a large number of candidates are eliminated by them</li><li>delegates (who make the final decision about the candidate) are chosen by them</li><li>they attract a large amount of media attention</li><li>lesser-known candidates see them as a way of boosting name recognition</li><li>they test some presidential skills (e.g. oratorical, presentational, organisational)</li><li>they are much more important than they used to be before the McGovern–Fraser reforms (1970s)</li></ul>	<ul><li>primaries often merely confirm decisions made during the 'invisible primary' (i.e. the candidates leading in the polls at the start of the primaries are often the ones eventually chosen)</li><li>what goes on in the media (e.g. televised candidate debates) is often more important</li><li>many presidential skills are not tested (e.g. ability to compromise, ability to work with Congress)</li><li>many primaries choose so few delegates that they cannot be regarded as important</li></ul>

Debate

Strengths and weaknesses/advantages and disadvantages of primaries

Strengths/advantages	Weaknesses/disadvantages
• Increased levels of participation by voters • Increased choice of candidates • Process opened up to outside candidates (e.g. Obama, Trump) • A gruelling race for a gruelling job	• Can lead to voter apathy • Voters are often unrepresentative • Process is too long, too expensive, too dominated by the media • Can develop into bitter personal battles • Lack of 'peer review' • Role of 'super-delegates' (Democrats)

Exam tip

When presenting strengths/weaknesses, advantages/disadvantages, pros/cons in an essay, make sure that the second half of your essay doesn't just knock down what you said in the first half. Remember that what some regard as strengths, others see as weaknesses (a good phrase to use in such an answer). Also, one specific factor might be both a strength and a weakness depending on one's point of view.

How to improve the nomination process

There are various ways in which the nomination process could be improved:

- Abolish the caucuses and replace them with primaries.
- Do away with closed primaries, thereby increasing voter eligibility.
- Rotate the order of primaries to increase geographic and demographic diversity.
- Tie super-delegate votes to the primary results in their respective states. (The Democrats are expected to make some changes about super-delegates before 2020.)
- Allow candidates to select their own delegates rather than having them allocated by the state party.
- Institute four regional primaries, held on the first Tuesdays of March, April, May and June.
- Hold a national primary.

Choosing vice presidential candidates

REVISED

The vice presidential candidate is chosen by the presidential candidate or by the incumbent president (when seeking re-election).

- The nomination needs to be confirmed by a majority vote of delegates at the national party convention.
- It used to be announced at the national party convention, but now is announced before that.
- It is a big media event, especially when there's an element of surprise.
- The announcement can give the presidential candidate a boost in the polls.
- Candidates use different strategies for choosing their running-mate:
  - a **balanced ticket**, e.g. Obama–Biden (2008), McCain–Palin (2012)
  - potential for government, e.g. Bush–Cheney (2000), Trump–Pence (2016)
  - party unity, e.g. Reagan–Bush (1980), Kerry–Edwards (2004).

Balanced ticket: A pairing of presidential and vice presidential candidates on a ticket, who attract support for different reasons, thereby making the broadest appeal to voters.

Now test yourself

TESTED

7 What is the difference between a primary and a caucus?
8 What are the two functions of primaries?
9 Explain the terms (a) Super Tuesday and (b) front loading.
10 What is the difference between an open and a closed primary?
11 What is the difference between a proportional and a winner-take-all primary?
12 What happens in the primaries when an incumbent president is running for re-election?
13 What is turnout like in primaries and caucuses?
14 Give three reasons why primaries (a) are and (b) are not important.
15 Give (a) three strengths and (b) three weaknesses of primaries.

Answers on pp. 115–16

National party conventions

REVISED

National party conventions are held by Democrats and Republicans as well as by some third parties.

- They are usually held during July or August.
- The challenging party (the one not controlling the White House) holds its convention first.
- A convention usually lasts for 3–4 days.
- It is held in a large city, usually in the East or Midwest (because of the time difference), e.g. 2016 – Republicans in Cleveland, Ohio; Democrats in Philadelphia, Pennsylvania. The 2020 Republican Convention will be held in Charlotte, North Carolina.
- The convention is attended by delegates, most of whom were chosen in the primaries and caucuses.
- Conventions have three formal functions:
  - choosing the presidential candidate (but in effect merely confirming the decision made during the primaries)
  - choosing the vice presidential candidate (but in effect merely confirming the choice announced earlier)
  - deciding the party platform – that is, the policy document upon which the election will be fought (but in effect merely ratifying the document drawn up earlier by the party's platform committee).
- So it's the informal functions that are more significant:
  - promoting party unity
  - enthusing the party faithful (the attendees)
  - enthusing ordinary voters (watching the key events on television or on line).
- The key moment is the presidential candidate's acceptance speech, which is still covered by major TV networks.
- The candidate hopes for post-convention 'bounce' in the polls as a result of the convention (but Trump's post-convention bounce in 2016 was just 1 percentage point).

> **National party convention:** The meeting held every four years by each of the two major parties to select presidential and vice presidential candidates and to agree the party platform.

> **Exam tip**
>
> Don't say that 'the conventions choose the presidential candidates' without explaining more carefully what you mean by that.

Debate

Are national party conventions still important?

Yes	No
• The only time the national parties meet together • Provide an opportunity to promote party unity after the primaries • Provide an opportunity to enthuse the party faithful to go and campaign for the ticket • Introduce the presidential candidates to the public • Delivery of the acceptance speech • Can lead to a significant 'bounce' in the polls • Many voters don't tune in to the campaign until the conventions start • A significant number of voters make their decision about who to vote for at this stage	• Nowadays they make few (if any) significant decisions; merely confirm decisions made earlier that we already know about • Television coverage has become much reduced • Ordinary voters don't really see them as important • Those held when the party is nominating the sitting president for re-election can be devoid of any real significance • More balloons, hoopla and celebrities than serious policy debate and presentation

Now test yourself

TESTED

16 What are the three formal functions of national party conventions?
17 Give three informal functions of the conventions.
18 Give three reasons why the conventions (a) are and (b) are not important.

Answers on p. 116

The general election campaign

REVISED

This is when the inter-party contest begins.
- It began traditionally on Labor Day (first Monday in September) – though these days it begins straight after the conventions – and lasts until early November.
- It is a nine-week campaign.
- It is fought mainly in the media but with the candidates making campaign appearances in key states.
- Candidates can be hit by an unforeseen problem that damages their campaign late on – the '**October surprise**' – which gives them little or no time to recover, e.g. in 2000, press disclosure that Bush had a drink-driving conviction; in 2016, FBI director Comey's re-opening of an investigation into Clinton's use of a private e-mail server while she was secretary of state.

> **October surprise:** An event occurring late in the presidential campaign to the disadvantage of one candidate, leaving that candidate with little or no time to recover before Election Day.

Campaign finance

The Federal Election Campaign Act (1974):
- A direct result of the Watergate scandal.
- Limited contributions that individuals, unions and corporations could give.
- But loopholes found.
- Saw the rise in '**soft money**'.
- Also weakened by the Supreme Court decision in 1976 (*Buckley v Valeo*) and subsequent congressional legislation.
- Provided matching funds administered by the newly created Federal Election Commission (FEC).

> **Soft money:** Money donated to political parties instead of to candidates to avoid campaign finance limitations. Parties are allowed to spend the money on certain campaigning activities such as voter registration and get-out-the-vote drives.

- These funds dominated presidential campaigns between 1976 and 2004.
- In 2008, Obama opted out of matching funds, leaving him free from limits on money raising and spending.
- In 2012 and 2016, both candidates opted out of matching funds.

The Bipartisan Campaign Reform Act (BICRA) (2002):
- Often referred to as the McCain–Feingold Act, after its two initiators, Republican John McCain and Democrat Russell Feingold, both senators.
- 2004 election saw the appearance of '527s', named after the section of the US tax code under which they operate.
- Also led to the further widespread use of **political action committees (PACs)**.
- Supreme Court decision in 2010 (*Citizens United v FEC*) granted corporate and labour organisations the same rights of political free speech – and therefore political fundraising – as individuals and led to setting up of expenditure-only committees, popularly known as **Super PACs**.

The main provisions of BICRA are:
- national party committees are banned from raising or spending 'soft money'
- labour unions and corporations are forbidden from directly funding issue ads
- unions and corporations are forbidden from financing ads that mention a federal candidate within 60 days of a general election or 30 days of a primary
- an increase in individual limits on contributions to individual candidates or candidate committees
- a ban on contributions from foreign nationals
- provides for a 'stand by your ad' verbal endorsement by candidates on TV ads.

Money raised by candidates, campaigns, PACs and Super PACS is spent on:
- organisation, manpower, and opening and running offices, mainly in swing states
- get-out-the-vote operations on Election Day
- campaigning, including travel and accommodation costs
- media, including buying time for political ads on TV and internet.

> **Political action committee (PAC)**: A political committee that raises limited amounts of money and spends these contributions for the express purpose of electing or defeating candidates.
>
> **Super PAC**: A political committee that makes independent expenditures, but does not make contributions to candidates.

> **Exam tip**
>
> Be careful when writing about the importance of money. It is somewhat misleading to say that someone 'needs a lot of money' to run for the presidency. You don't have to possess vast personal wealth to be successful. Neither Clinton (1992) nor Obama (2008) was particularly wealthy. Say, rather, that someone 'needs to raise a lot of money' to run successfully for the presidency.

Televised debates

Televised debates began in 1960, but then there were none until 1976. However, they have been held in each election since then.
- Nowadays there are usually three presidential debates and one vice presidential debate.
- The non-partisan Commission on Presidential Debates was set up in 1987 to sponsor and organise the debates.
- Only major party candidates are invited to participate (except in 1980 and 1992 when third-party candidates – John Anderson and Ross Perot respectively – were invited).
- Different styles of debates have been used:
  - candidates at podiums with either a panel of questioners or just one moderator
  - town hall style with the audience asking some/all of the questions
  - round table discussion with the candidates sat around a table with the moderator.

Debate

Are the televised presidential debates important?

Yes	No
<ul><li>They can play a decisive role in the campaign (e.g. 1980, 2012)</li><li>They can affect the opinion polls</li><li>They are especially important for the challenging candidate, who will be less well known</li><li>A good sound bite from a candidate will be played repeatedly in the media in the days that follow</li><li>A gaffe can seriously affect a candidate's chances of success (e.g. Gore in 2000)</li></ul>	<ul><li>In 2016, polls found that Clinton easily won all three debates, yet she lost the election</li><li>Trump's numerous debate gaffes did not seriously affect his poll numbers</li><li>Policy detail is rarely discussed</li><li>They are not really 'debates', more the trotting out of rehearsed lines and catch-phrases</li><li>Viewership has tended to decline (though it was up in 2016)</li></ul>

Now test yourself

TESTED

19 When does the general election campaign traditionally begin?
20 How long does the general election campaign last?
21 What is an 'October surprise'?
22 What is a political action committee (PAC)?
23 Give three main provisions of the Bipartisan Campaign Reform Act (2002).
24 Who now sponsors and organises the presidential debates?
25 Name three different styles of debate that have been used.
26 Give three reasons why these debates are important.
27 Give three reasons why these debates are not important.

Answers on pp. 116–17

Election Day

REVISED

Election Day is fixed by federal law as the Tuesday after the first Monday in November (falls between 2 and 8 November).

- But more than 30 states permit early voting – it is estimated that some 47 million voted early in 2016.
- Voter turnout peaked at 67% in 1960 and then dropped steadily to reach 51% in 1996.
- Turnout increased in 2000, 2004 and 2008, but was back down to around 54% in 2016.
- It is very difficult to defeat incumbent presidents seeking a second term (see Table 6.1).
- The three who lost all faced significant opposition in the primaries – Ford, for instance, was an unelected president; Bush had already served eight years as vice president as well as four years as president.

Table 6.1 Presidents seeking re-election: 1956–2012

Year	President seeking re-election	Party	Result
1956	Dwight Eisenhower	R	Won
1964	Lyndon Johnson	D	Won
1972	Richard Nixon	R	Won
1976	Gerald Ford	R	Lost
1980	Jimmy Carter	D	Lost
1984	Ronald Reagan	R	Won
1992	George H.W. Bush	R	Lost
1996	Bill Clinton	D	Won
2004	George W. Bush	R	Won
2012	Barack Obama	D	Won

Now test yourself

TESTED

28 What does federal law state about the date of the election?
29 How many states allowed early voting in 2016?
30 What has happened to voter turnout in recent decades?
31 How many incumbent presidents have been defeated since the 1950s? Who were they?

Answers on p. 117

Electoral College voting

REVISED

How it works

- The president is not elected by the popular vote but through the **Electoral College**.
- Each state is awarded a certain number of Electoral College votes (ECVs).
- The number is equal to that state's representation in Congress – the number of senators (two) plus the number of representatives.
- Thus Wyoming has 3 ECVs (2 + 1); California has 55 (2 + 53).
- There are 538 ECVs altogether.
- A candidate needs an absolute majority (270) to win the presidency.
- The popular votes are counted in each state.
- The winner of the popular vote in a state wins all that state's ECVs – the so-called 'winner-take-all' rule.
- This 'rule' is not in the Constitution, only in state law.
- Two states – Maine and Nebraska – do not use the winner-take-all rule.
- The members of the Electoral College never meet together.
- Its members (Electors) meet in their respective state capitals on the Monday after the second Wednesday in December to cast their ballots for president and vice president.
- They send their results to the vice president, who formally counts and announces the Electoral College votes in Congress in early January.
- If no candidate wins an overall majority:
  - the president is elected by the House of Representatives (one vote per state delegation), with 26 votes (out of 50) required to win
  - the vice president is elected by the Senate, with 51 votes (out of 100) required to win.
- This has occurred only twice: in 1800 and 1824.

> **Electoral College:** The institution established by the Founding Fathers to indirectly elect the president and vice president. The Electors cast their ballots in their state capitals.

> **Typical mistake**
>
> You must say an *absolute* majority – that is, more than everyone else put together: 50% + 1.

> **Exam tip**
>
> You really do need to know how the Electoral College works. So learn it! Too many candidates just don't.

Strengths and weaknesses

The strengths and weaknesses of the Electoral College are outlined in Table 6.2.

Table 6.2 Strengths and weaknesses (advantages/disadvantages) of the Electoral College

Strengths/advantages	Weaknesses/disadvantages
● Preserves the voice of the small-population states (Table 6.3) ● Usually promotes a two-horse race, with the winner receiving more than 50% of the popular vote (Table 6.4)	● Small-population states are over-represented ● The winner-take-all system can distort the result ● It is possible for the loser of the popular vote to win the Electoral College vote (Table 6.4) ● It is unfair to national third parties (Table 6.5) ● There may be **rogue or faithless Electors** (Table 6.6) ● There is a potential problem if the Electoral College is deadlocked

Table 6.3 Number of people per Electoral College vote: five smallest and five largest states (thousands)

State	Number of people per Electoral College vote (thousands)
Five smallest-population states	
Wyoming	195
Vermont	208
Alaska	247
North Dakota	253
South Dakota	288
Five largest-population states	
Illinois	640
New York	679
Florida	710
California	713
Texas	734

Rogue/faithless Electors: An Elector in the Electoral College who casts their ballot for a candidate other than the one who won the popular vote in their state.

Table 6.4 Popular vote percentage of winning candidate, 1980–2016 (popular vote winner in bold)

Year	Winning candidate	Winner's popular vote (%)	Loser's popular vote (%)
1980	Ronald Reagan (R)	**50.7**	41.0
1984	Ronald Reagan (R)	**58.8**	40.6
1988	George H.W. Bush (R)	**53.4**	45.6
1992	Bill Clinton (D)	**43.0**	37.4
1996	Bill Clinton (D)	**49.2**	40.7
2000	George W. Bush (R)	47.9	**48.4**
2004	George W. Bush (R)	**50.7**	48.3
2008	Barack Obama (D)	**52.9**	45.7
2012	Barack Obama (D)	**51.1**	47.2
2016	Donald Trump (R)	46.1	**48.2**

Table 6.5 1992 presidential election: popular vote and Electoral College vote compared

Candidate	Party	Popular vote (%)	Electoral College votes
Bill Clinton	D	43.0	370
George H.W. Bush	R	37.4	168
Ross Perot	Independent	18.9	0

Table 6.6 Faithless presidential Electors, 2016

State	To match the popular vote, Elector should have voted for:	Elector actually voted for:
Hawaii	Hillary Clinton	Bernie Sanders
Texas	Donald Trump	John Kasich
	Donald Trump	Ron Paul
Washington	Hillary Clinton	Colin Powell
	Hillary Clinton	Colin Powell
	Hillary Clinton	Colin Powell
	Hillary Clinton	Faith Spotted Eagle

Possible reforms

Direct election

Following 2000 and 2016 when the loser of the popular vote won the election, calls were made for the president to be elected by popular vote.

But this reform would have problems of its own:
- With a multiplicity of candidates, it was unlikely that the winner would gain 50% of the vote.
- There was a possible need, therefore, for a run-off election between the top two – further prolonging an already lengthy process.
- This could be brought about only by a Constitutional amendment – which is highly unlikely.

Congressional district system

This system is currently used in Maine and Nebraska.
- One ECV is allocated to the winner in each congressional district.
- Two ECVs are allocated to the state-wide winner.
- In 2016, Maine split its ECVs – Clinton 3, Trump 1.
- But this reform would also have problems of its own:
  - In 2000, it would have made the result even less proportionate: Bush would have won 288 ECVs on the basis of 47.9% of the popular vote.
  - In 2012, Romney would have won the election on this system on just 47.2% of the popular vote.

Proportional system

Each state would allocate ECVs in exact proportion to that state's popular vote.
- This would render the Electors unnecessary.
- It would be much fairer to national third parties.
- But that would make it far more difficult for any one candidate to gain 50% of the vote.

- Therefore, there would be a need for a run-off election (see above).
- So, for all its flaws, the current system seems likely to remain because:
  - there is no widespread consensus on a better alternative
  - it is highly unlikely that any significant reform would be legislatively or Constitutionally doable
  - the suggested reforms also have significant problems.
- After these seven stages and more than a calendar year of campaigning and voting, the president is sworn into office on 20 January of the following year.

Now test yourself

TESTED

32 How are the Electoral College votes (ECVs) allocated among the 50 states?
33 How many ECVs does a candidate need to win the presidency?
34 How do most states allocate their ECVs?
35 Which are the states that don't? How do they do it?
36 What are 'rogue' or 'faithless' Electors? Give an example from 2016.
37 What are the two strengths of the Electoral College?
38 Give four of the weaknesses of the Electoral College.
39 Name three possible reforms that are suggested.
40 Give two reasons why the current system is likely to remain in place.

Answers on p. 117

Congressional elections

See also Chapter 2.

When congressional elections occur

REVISED

- House members are elected every two years.
- Senators are elected for six-year terms, with one-third being up for re-election every two years.
- So in each two-year cycle of congressional elections, all of the House and one-third of the Senate are up for re-election.
- The elections are held on the Tuesday after the first Monday in November.
- In years divisible by four (2016, 2020, 2024, etc.) they coincide with the presidential election.
- Elections in the years between presidential elections (2014, 2018, 2022, etc.) are called **midterm elections** as they fall midway through the president's four-year term of office.

Exam tip

To avoid confusion, use the term 'House members' to refer to members of the House of Representatives.

Midterm elections: Elections for the whole of the House and one-third of the Senate that occur midway through a president's four-year term.

Requirements for a congressional candidate

REVISED

Candidates for the House of Representatives:
- at least 25 years old
- an American citizen for at least seven years
- resident of the state they represent
- some states also include a **locality rule**.

Candidates for the Senate:
- at least 30 years old
- an American citizen for at least nine years
- resident of the state they represent.

Locality rule: A state law that requires House members to be resident in the congressional district they represent.

Nomination process

Nomination is secured through congressional primaries.
- They are held between May and September of each election year.
- Winner of the primary becomes the party's House/Senate candidate.
- Incumbents rarely face a serious challenge.
- In a 34-year period (1982–2016), only 8 senators and 72 House members were defeated in primaries.

Trends in congressional elections

It is possible to discern five important trends in congressional elections:

The power of incumbency is significant

- Between 2000 and 2016, House re-election rates ranged from 85% (2010) to 98% (2000).
- During the same period, Senate re-election rates ranged from 79% (2006) to 96% (2004).
- Most members of Congress leave by voluntary retirement or through seeking election to higher office rather than by electoral defeat.
- Reasons for high rates of re-election include:
  - their ability to provide federal funding for constituency/state projects
  - high levels of name recognition
  - fundraising advantages: incumbents can usually raise much more than challengers can.

The coattails effect is limited

The **coattails effect** was last seen to be very strong in 1980 – Republican Ronald Reagan helped win 33 House seats and 12 Senate seats.

There was some coattails effect for Republican Donald Trump in the 2016 Senate races: three incumbent Republicans won seats they were expected to lose in states where Trump ran unexpectedly well.

Split-ticket voting is declining

The number of congressional districts that voted for a presidential candidate of one party and a House member from the other party (**split-ticket voting**) declined from 196 (1984) to 35 (2016).

The number of states voting for a presidential candidate of one party and a senator from the other party declined from 6 out of 34 (2004) to zero (2016).

There are fewer competitive House districts

A competitive district is one in which the winner won by less than 10 percentage points at the previous election.
- The number has fallen from 111 (1992) to 31 (2016).
- This is significant because:
  - it makes it much harder for party control of the House to change hands
  - members from safe districts are more likely to cast party-line votes than are those from competitive ones
  - it therefore increases levels of partisanship.

> **Coattails effect**: The effect when an extremely popular candidate at the top of the ticket (e.g. for president or governor) carries candidates for lower offices with him/her into office.
>
> **Split-ticket voting**: Voting for candidates of two or more parties for different offices at the same election (the opposite of **straight-ticket voting**).
>
> **Straight-ticket voting**: Voting for candidates of the same party for different offices at the same election.

> **Exam tip**
>
> It is easy to give the impression that partisanship is, in itself, a bad thing. But politicians sticking to what they believe and to what they promised in their campaigns is not necessarily bad. Indeed, some voters will want them to do just that!

The president's party tends to lose seats in midterm elections

In the six midterm elections in the period 1994–2014, the president's party lost an average of 25 House seats and around 4–5 in the Senate.

- In the House, this ranged from a gain of 5 seats (1998, 2002) to a loss of 63 (2010).
- In the Senate, this ranged from a gain of 2 seats (2002) to a loss of 9 (2014).
- The reasons include:
  - without the winning presidential candidate on the ticket, House members from the president's party do less well
  - voters see midterms as an opportunity to register disappointment/ disapproval with the president.

Now test yourself

TESTED

41 In each two-year election cycle, what proportions of the House and the Senate are up for re-election?
42 What are midterm elections?
43 How do the qualifications for the House differ from those for the Senate?
44 What is the locality rule?
45 Give two reasons for the high rates of re-election in Congress.
46 What is the coattails effect?
47 What is split-ticket voting?
48 Give two ways in which the decline in competitive House districts may be significant.
49 Give two reasons why the president's party tends to lose seats in Congress in the midterm elections.

Answers on p. 117

Summary

You should now have an understanding of:
- requirements for presidential candidates
- the invisible primary
- presidential primaries
- the selection of vice presidential candidates
- national party conventions
- the general election campaign
- the Electoral College
- congressional elections
- midterm elections

Exam practice

Note: This specification does not include a comparison between US and UK elections or electoral systems.

Section C (USA)

In your answer you must consider the stated view and the alternative to this view in a balanced way.
1 Evaluate the extent to which presidential primaries are important. [30]
2 Evaluate the extent to which the Electoral College is in need of reform. [30]

Answers and quick quiz online

ONLINE

7 Parties and pressure groups

Party organisation

Organisation of US political parties reflects the federal structure of government.

Parties are largely decentralised – organised mainly at the state level.

Think of them as 50 state Democratic and 50 state Republican parties, plus a national committee for each party.

Developments since the 1970s

REVISED ☐

Since the 1970s, a number of factors have led to strengthening of national party structures:
- New campaign finance laws resulted in money flowing to the national parties and the candidates themselves rather than being raised by the state or local parties.
- Television provided a medium through which candidates could appeal directly to voters, thereby cutting out state and local parties that had traditionally been the medium.
- Emergence of sophisticated opinion polls allowed candidates to directly 'hear' what voters were saying without actually meeting them.
- New technology allowed national parties to set up sophisticated fundraising and direct mailing operations – later also via social media.
- Parties became more ideologically cohesive.
- National parties played a larger role in recruitment and training of congressional candidates.

All this meant that party organisation became more top-down rather than bottom-up.

Current state of play

REVISED ☐

Each party has a national committee with offices in Washington DC. But members are representatives from the 50 state parties.
- Headed by national chair – mostly rather anonymous bureaucrats who are seldom in the public eye.
- National party conventions – held in each presidential election year (every four years).
- Also congressional party leadership with committees to oversee policy-making and campaigning.
- State parties headed by state party chairs – hold state party conventions.
- Grassroots level: congressional district, county, city, ward and precinct level organisation.

> **Exam tip**
>
> In the USA, the Republican Party is often referred to as 'the GOP' – short for 'the Grand Old Party'. It's a useful essay abbreviation.

Now test yourself

TESTED

1 What is the main reason why US political parties are decentralised?
2 What organisation do the Democrats and Republicans have at the national level?
3 Give three factors that have led to the strengthening of national party structures.
4 Who heads the national parties?
5 What organisation exists below the national level?

Answers on pp. 117–18

Party ideology

The names suggest that they are not ideologically exclusive parties. So ideological adjectives are often attached, e.g. 'conservative Republicans', 'liberal Democrats'. Bush (2000) ran as a 'compassionate conservative'.

The ideology is often linked to a geographic region, e.g. conservative South, liberal West Coast.

> **Typical mistake**
>
> Don't get the punctuation wrong in 'liberal Democrats' – liberal (lower case), Democrats (capital). Likewise, 'conservative Republicans'.

Growth of ideological differences

REVISED

The two major parties used to be ideologically wide and all-embracing: 'broad churches' was a popular phrase.

When asked 'Do you think there are any important differences in what Republicans and Democrats stand for?'
- In 1972: 46% said 'yes'; 44% said 'no'.
- In 2012: 81% said 'yes'; 18% said 'no'.

> **Ideology**: A collectively held set of beliefs.

When asked 'Is one party more conservative than the other?'
- In 1984: 53% said, 'yes, the Republicans'; 32% said 'no, both the same'.
- In 2012: 73% said 'yes, the Republicans'; 18% said 'no, both the same'.

The Democrats and ideology

REVISED

The two major parties are not ideological monoliths.
- Not all Democrats self-identify as liberals, especially in the South.
- Some will call themselves 'moderate' or 'conservative' Democrats.
- Many saw the 2016 Democratic presidential primary contest between Hillary Clinton and Bernie Sanders in terms of ideology: Clinton more moderate, Sanders more liberal.
- But exit poll data did not show that: liberal Democrats preferred Clinton over Sanders by 53% to 46%.
- However, that may have been because liberal Democrats saw Clinton as the more likely of the two to defeat Trump.

The Republicans and ideology

REVISED

Likewise, in the Republican Party, not all self-identify as conservatives, especially in the Northeast and the West.

Some will qualify their conservatism, for example:
- 'social conservatives' – conservative on social, moral and religious issues such as abortion, same-sex marriage
- 'fiscal conservatives' – want to reduce the national debt and the federal budget deficit, as well as reduce federal government taxation and spending (associated with the Tea Party movement)

- 'compassionate conservatives' – seek to use traditional conservative beliefs in order to improve the lives of those who feel abandoned and neglected by government and society.

In the 2016 presidential primaries, Trump appeared as a post-ideological candidate in many ways:

- neither a traditional conservative like Senator Ted Cruz of Texas
- nor a traditional moderate like the party's previous presidential nominee, Mitt Romney of Massachusetts.

> **Typical mistake**
>
> The Tea Party is not a party! It's best described as a movement.

> **Exam tip**
>
> When talking of President Trump and his party's policies, you may be tempted to do so in a subjective fashion – either for or against. Always resist the temptation!

Now test yourself

TESTED ☐

6 Define the term 'ideology'.
7 What is the prevailing ideology of each of the two major parties?
8 What is the difference between 'social' and 'fiscal' conservatives within the Republican Party?

Answers on p. 118

Party policies

It is possible to discern some clear differences between two major parties in terms of policies.

Not, of course, that all supporters of either party have the same view on key policies, but there are discernible trends of support and opposition on key policies by the parties, such as:

- increased spending on social welfare programmes: Democrats support; Republicans oppose
- death penalty: Democrats oppose; Republicans support
- gun control: Democrats support; Republicans oppose
- high levels of defence spending: Democrats oppose; Republicans support
- stricter environmental controls: Democrats support; Republicans oppose
- stricter controls on immigration: Democrats oppose; Republicans support
- 'Obamacare': Democrats support; Republicans oppose.

As a general rule of thumb:

- Democrats tend to be more progressive on social and moral issues, as well as on law and order; they tend to favour greater federal governmental intervention in the economy and on social and welfare issues such as education and healthcare
- Republicans tend to focus more on individualism and limited government.

> **Exam tip**
>
> When using such material in your exam answers, always include a caveat that these are generalisations. Not all Democrats or Republicans support or oppose a certain policy.

Now test yourself

TESTED ☐

9 Identify four policies over which the majority of Democrats and Republicans hold differing views.
10 Which would you describe as the more 'progressive' party?
11 Which places more emphasis on 'limited government'?

Answers on p. 118

Coalitions of supporters

- American parties are best thought of as coalitions of interests.
- These coalitions are more narrowly drawn than they were three or four decades ago.
- But both parties still need to put together a winning electoral coalition in order to win the presidency.
- Figure 7.1 shows groups among which the Republicans won the majority of votes in 2016.

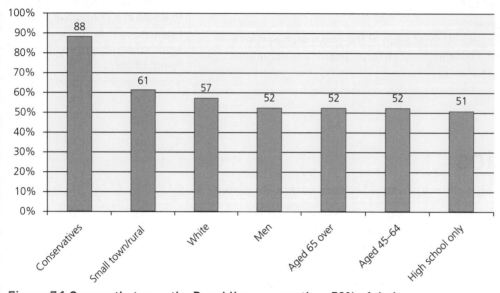

Figure 7.1 Groups that gave the Republicans more than 50% of their votes, 2016

- In the same election, the Democrats won the majority of votes among the groups shown in Figure 7.2.

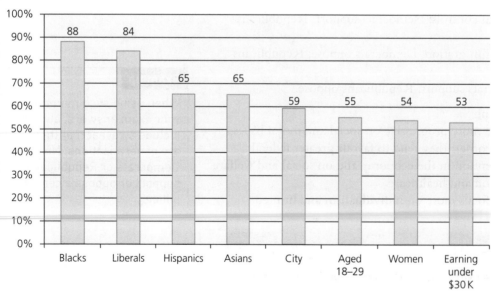

Figure 7.2 Groups that gave the Democrats more than 50% of their votes, 2016

Gender

REVISED

One has to go back to the Reagan landslide of 1984 to find an election in which the Republicans won a majority among women voters.

- Trump's 41% among women voters was the party's lowest in a two-candidate race since Barry Goldwater's 38% back in 1964.
- In 2016 the **gender gap** for Trump was 11 points: he won the votes of 52% of men but of just 41% of women.
- Trump was running against the first woman presidential candidate for a major party.
- He was not helped by the numerous stories of his treatment of women that emerged during the campaign.
- Among non-married women, Trump's support fell to 32%.

The Republican Party's trend of poor showing among women voters is generally thought to be linked with policy differences between the two major parties.

The Democrats tend to take policy positions more favoured by women on:
- abortion rights (support)
- capital punishment (oppose)
- gun control (support)
- lower levels of defence spending (support).

> **Gender gap**: The gap between the support given to a candidate by women and the support given to the same candidate by men.

> **Exam tip**
>
> The same warning about over-generalisation is relevant throughout this section. Many women vote Republican, as do many Catholics and some Hispanics. Likewise, significant numbers of men vote Democrat, as do many older voters and those living in small towns.

Race

REVISED

The most significant minority groups in terms of the numbers who vote are African-Americans and Hispanics/Latinos.
- Both give the majority of their votes to the Democrats – African-Americans overwhelmingly so.
- Hillary Clinton won the support of 89% of African-American voters in 2016.
- Hispanics are a growing group and therefore will continue to become an increasingly important voting group.
- Although they give a majority of their votes to Democratic candidates, George W. Bush won 43% among Hispanics in 2004.
- However, that was down to 28% for Trump in 2016.

Class and education

REVISED

Class and education have become increasingly important determinants of voting, especially in 2016, because an increasingly disillusioned group of voters, distinguished by class and education, cast their votes for Donald Trump.

They were disillusioned because:
- they felt neglected by Washington politicians of both parties who had made promises to them during campaigns but had failed to deliver once elected
- of the effects of the 2008–09 economic crash – they believed that whereas the government bailed out banks and big business, they were left unemployed and unhelped
- they believed that their values, way of life and beliefs (e.g. in traditional marriage) had been swept aside and sneered at by a 'liberal elite'
- they felt that the America in which they grew up – overwhelmingly white and nominally Christian – was fast disappearing.

The group that most typifies these voters are white, older, blue-collar, non-college-educated voters who live predominantly in the Rust Belt states of the Northeast and the Midwest:

- White, non-college-educated voters made up over one third of the 2016 electorate and voted 66% for Trump – 71% among men in this group, 61% among women.
- They were attracted by Trump's 'Make America Great Again' slogan.
- These are the so-called 'Trump base' – his core, loyal supporters.
- They are quite similar to '**Reagan Democrats**' in the 1980s.

> **Reagan Democrats**: White, working-class voters, mostly living in the Northeast and the Midwest, who had been traditional Democrats but who supported Republican Ronald Reagan in 1980 and 1984.

Geographic region

REVISED

There are four important trends when it comes to geographic voting:
1. The Northeast has become a Democratic stronghold (notwithstanding the defection of many white, non-college-educated voters to Trump in 2016).
2. The South, having been solid for the Democrats, in the last three decades has become solidly Republican.
3. The West Coast continues to be a Democratic stronghold.
4. A swathe of states running from Idaho through the Dakotas, Montana, Wyoming, Kansas and Missouri have become increasingly solid for the Republicans.

All this means that presidential elections are won or lost in a handful of swing states such as Florida, Ohio, Virginia and North Carolina.

Religion

REVISED

- Protestants, and especially white evangelicals, vote predominantly for Republicans.
- Catholics traditionally support Democrats.
- Those who more regularly and frequently attend a church are more likely to vote Republican.
- Those who rarely or never attend are more likely to vote Democratic.

Now test yourself

TESTED

12 Identify four groups that gave a majority of their votes to the Republicans in 2016.
13 Identify four groups that gave a majority of their votes to the Democrats in 2016.
14 Explain the term 'the gender gap'.
15 Give three reasons why Democrats traditionally win a majority of votes among women voters.
16 Give three reasons why older, white, blue-collar, non-college-educated voters felt disillusioned going into the 2016 election.
17 What was it about Donald Trump's campaign that appealed to these voters?
18 Name three 'swing states'.
19 What pointers are there in religion regarding party support?

Answers on p. 118

The polarisation of American politics

The 1990s brought a significant ideological shift in American politics.

- Both parties became more ideologically cohesive: the Democrats more liberal, the Republicans much more conservative.
- The nation became divided into what commentators called 'Blue America' and 'Red America' – referring to the colours the TV networks use to colour maps on election night: blue for Democrats, red for Republicans.

Exam tip

When discussing polarisation and 'Blue America' and 'Red America', always make it clear that these are only trends and generalisations, but nonetheless they are useful indicators.

Red America: characterised as:	Blue America: characterised as:
• predominantly white • overwhelmingly Protestant (and especially evangelical) • rural, small town or suburban • fiscally and socially conservative • pro-guns • pro-life • pro-traditional marriage • supporting limited role for federal government • opposed to Obamacare • viewers of Fox News	• a racial rainbow of white, black, Asian, Hispanic/Latino • urban • socially liberal • supporting gun control measures • pro-choice • pro-gay rights • supporting an expansive role for federal government • supporting Obamacare • watching CNN and *Saturday Night Live*

Now test yourself

TESTED

20 Give five characteristics of typical voters in 'Red America'.
21 Give five characteristics of typical voters in 'Blue America'.

Answers on p. 118

The two-party system

Evidence of a two-party system

REVISED

1 Popular vote – in all the last seven presidential elections, two major parties have won more than 80% of the popular vote, on four occasions exceeding 95%.
2 Congressional seats – after 2016, two major parties controlled 533 of the 535 seats in Congress (senators Angus King and Bernie Sanders being the two exceptions, though both vote with the Democrats).
3 Executive branch control – every president since 1853 has been a Democrat or a Republican.
4 State government – by 2017, 49 of the 50 state governors were either Democrats or Republicans (Bill Walker of Alaska is an independent).

Two-party system: A party system in which two major parties regularly win the vast majority of votes, capture nearly all of the seats in the legislature and alternately control the executive.

Reasons for a two-party system

REVISED

1 Electoral system – the first-past-the-post electoral system makes life very difficult for national third parties.
2 Broad party ideologies – there is very little room for other parties, except at the ideological fringes.
3 Primary elections – these make the two major parties more responsive to the electorate, thereby minimising the need for protest voting.

Typical mistake

A two-party system is not a system with only two parties!

Now test yourself

TESTED

22 Define a two-party system.
23 Give three pieces of evidence that suggest that the USA has a two-party system.
24 Give three reasons why the USA has a two-party system.

Answers on pp. 118–19

Third parties

Despite the domination of the two major parties, third parties do exist.

There are different types:
- national, e.g. Libertarian Party, Green Party
- regional, e.g. George Wallace's American Independent Party in 1968
- state-based, e.g. New York Conservative Party.

Some are permanent (e.g. Green Party, Libertarian Party); others are temporary (e.g. Reform Party, 1996).

Some are issues-based (e.g. Green Party, Constitution Party – formerly the Taxpayers' Party); others are ideological (e.g. Socialist Party, Libertarian Party).

Impact of third parties

REVISED

Third parties might be thought to have little or no impact at all as they rarely win a significant number of votes.

Nevertheless, they might be thought to have some significant impact in that they can:
- influence the outcome even with a very small percentage of the votes (e.g. 2000)
- influence the policy agenda of the two major parties (e.g. the Green Party).

Third parties can have some impact within certain states (e.g. the Green Party won 9% of the vote in the 2010 midterms in South Carolina).

Do third parties play any significant role in US politics?

Yes	No
● Ross Perot won 19% of the vote in 1992, thereby contributing to the defeat of President George H.W. Bush ● The Green Party's 2.7% in 2000 contributed to Al Gore's defeat ● Although third parties lose the electoral battle, they can win the policy battle by making one/both of the major parties co-opt their policies in order to win back their voters ● Some states (e.g. Alaska, New York) have vibrant third parties	● The two major parties dominate all presidential elections ● Third parties are usually excluded from the TV debates during the presidential campaign (except Perot in 1992) ● The two major parties dominate and control Congress ● The two major parties dominate state politics

Difficulties facing third parties

1 Electoral system: the first-past-the-post, winner-take-all system makes it very difficult for third parties to win.
2 Ballot access laws: third parties are disadvantaged by laws regulating how candidates must qualify for the ballot in each of the 50 states.
3 Lack of resources: difficulties in raising significant amounts of money result in little to spend on campaigning, advertising, organisation, get-out-the-vote operations.
4 Lack of media coverage: not newsworthy; cannot afford TV advertising; excluded from TV debates.
5 Co-optation of their policies: major parties may co-opt their policies, thereby depriving them of future success (e.g. Democrat Bill Clinton's co-optation of Perot's flagship policy from 1992 relating to the federal budget deficit).

Exam tip

Examiners may hint at third parties sometimes being seen to be the 'winners' when they set a question such as 'Evaluate the extent to which third parties always lose in presidential elections.' In answering that question, you need to differentiate between third parties always losing the election but sometimes winning the policy argument when their policies are co-opted by one or both of the major parties.

Now test yourself TESTED

25 Identify three different types of third parties, giving an example of each.
26 Give two ways in which third parties might be said to have a significant impact on politics in the USA.
27 Identify three difficulties that face third parties in the USA.

Answers on p. 119

Current conflicts within the parties

The Democrats REVISED

After eight years of Obama in the White House (2009–17), the Democrats were in a much weaker position than they had been when Obama was first elected.
● They lost the presidential election in 2016 – though their candidate won nearly 3 million more votes than her opponent.

- From 2008 to 2016 they lost 10 seats in the Senate and 61 in the House, losing control of both chambers.
- During the same period the number of Democrat governors fell from 29 to 16.
- They lost nearly 1,000 state legislative seats during the same eight-year period.
- At state level, the party in 2017 was at its lowest electoral level since 1925.

This led to conflict between the more left-of-centre, liberal Democrats – the Bernie Sanders wing – and the more centrist, establishment wing represented by Hillary Clinton and the party's congressional leadership team.

The election of Tom Perez as chair of the Democratic National Committee was seen by Sanders as a victory for the 'failed status quo approach'.

This all means that the party's presidential nomination race ahead of the 2020 election will be especially keenly fought.

The Republicans

REVISED

Meanwhile, a similar split had developed in the Republican Party.
- This initially showed itself in the appearance of the Tea Party movement and then developed into the so-called Freedom Caucus, made up of around three dozen House Republicans led by Rep. Mark Meadows advocating a conservative and libertarian agenda.
- The Freedom Caucus members were influential in ending the speakership of Republican John Boehner in 2015 and have proved influential in a number of key House votes, most notably those concerning the repeal and replacement of the Affordable Care Act (Obamacare).
- There has also been a split in the party between what one might call the traditional Republican Party establishment and the supporters of Donald Trump.
- The establishment versus Trump debate shows itself in debates concerning such issues as free trade versus protectionism, the environment, immigration control, and internationalism versus 'America First' nationalism.
- Both the 2018 midterms and the 2020 presidential election will give some indication of the balance of power within the party.

Now test yourself

TESTED

28 Give three pieces of evidence of the Democrats' electoral decline between 2009 and 2017.
29 Explain why this decline led to conflict within the party.
30 What splits have appeared within the Republican Party in the past decade?

Answers on p. 119

Exam practice answers and quick quizzes at **www.hoddereducation.co.uk/myrevisionnotesdownloads**

Comparing US and UK parties

Campaign finance and party funding

In both systems, scandals over election and party funding have led to widespread concern. This in turn has led to changes in the law. But then parties, groups and individuals often find ways around the new legislation.

In the USA, there is the added question of whether the new law is constitutional, often leading to a ruling by the Supreme Court (e.g. *McConnell v Federal Election Commission* (2004); *Citizens United v Federal Election Commission* (2010) – see Chapter 4).

Both the USA and the UK have tried state funding as a way to solve campaign and party funding problems:
- USA: federal matching funds were introduced in the 1970s.
- UK: the introduction of Short Money in the 1970s.

But in neither country has significant state funding of political parties been adopted and this is where the debate is to be found.

Debate

Should state funding for political parties be introduced?

Yes, because it would...	No, because it would...
<ul><li>end parties' dependence on wealthy donors</li><li>enable parties to better perform their democratic functions – organisation, representation, creating policy priorities</li><li>fill the gap created by falling membership</li><li>lead to greater transparency</li><li>help equalise parties' financial resources</li><li>make it easier to limit spending</li><li>encourage greater public engagement if funding were linked to electoral turnout</li></ul>	<ul><li>reinforce the financial advantage of major parties</li><li>further increase disconnect between parties and voters</li><li>diminish belief in the principle that citizen participation is voluntary</li><li>lead to objections from tax payers whose money would go to parties they don't support</li><li>reinforce the parties' role which many see as an anachronism in the digital age</li></ul>

Issues surrounding party funding can be interpreted in line with the structural theoretical approach:
- structures create relationships within institutions
- within parties, there is the relationship between the party establishment and the party members, donors and supporters.

This can also be interpreted in line with the rational choice approach:
- major party hierarchies will mostly be happy with the status quo
- third/minor parties will seek change
- but each favours the funding method that benefits their situation
- so the American Green and Libertarian parties and the UK Liberal Democrats are more likely to favour state funding than do the major parties in both countries.

Party systems

REVISED

Theories of party systems tend to distinguish between three overlapping formats:

- dominant-party systems: some US states, e.g. Wyoming, Massachusetts; some UK parliamentary constituencies – where one party almost always wins all elections
- two-party systems, e.g. the US party system
- multiparty systems, e.g. the UK party system.

As both the USA and the UK have a first-past-the-post electoral system at the national level, how is it that their respective party systems are so different?

- The UK, too, used to have a two-party system: in the 1955 general election the two major parties won over 96% of the vote.
- By 2015 that had fallen to 67%.
- After the 1955 election, there were just 4 parties represented in the House of Commons; by 2015 there were 11.

The answer lies in the cultural and structural changes that have occurred in the UK over the past six decades:

- the rise of nationalism in Scotland, leading to devolution and calls for independence from the Scottish National Party (SNP)
- the rise of nationalism in Wales, leading to devolution and increased support for Plaid Cymru (Welsh Nationalists)
- 'the troubles' in Northern Ireland, boosting support for nationalist parties in the province as well as splitting the Unionists away from the Conservative Party.

No such cultural and structural changes occurred in the USA.

Internal party unity

REVISED

Internal party unity can often be an issue for broad-church parties such as the two major parties in both the USA and the UK.

It is usually less of an issue for one-issue, nationalist, ideological third parties such as the Green Party or the SNP.

Party factions can be constructive (providing new ideas and policies) or destructive (party in-fighting for control of party agenda and leadership).

Party factions therefore have different aims and functions, such as to:

- accentuate certain policies (e.g. income inequality, low taxes, moral issues)
- focus on a particular ideological aspect (e.g. conservative Democrats, hard left, libertarians)
- reflect geographic, ethnic, economic, generational, religious groups (e.g. southern Democrats, Christian Right, one-nation Conservatives)
- widen voter appeal (e.g. Tea Party, Momentum)
- extol the party 'greats' (e.g. Reaganites, Thatcherites, Bennites)
- challenge the party establishment (e.g. Freedom Caucus, New Labour, Tea Party, Corbynistas).

Party policies

REVISED

Differences in the historical background to the major parties is key.

- Unlike the Democratic Party in the USA, the British Labour Party came out of the trade union movement and has been closely linked with socialism.

- Unlike the Republican Party in the USA, the British Conservative Party grew out of a landed aristocracy and the established church.

Nevertheless, there are a number of broad policy agreements between the Republicans and the Conservatives. Both:
- dislike 'big government'
- favour low taxation
- talk of being strong on law and order
- stress high levels of defence spending
- talk more about equality of opportunity than equality of results.

Similarly, there are a number of broad policy agreements between the Democrats and Labour. Both:
- put great stress on the rights of minorities – gender, racial, sexual orientation
- stress the rights of workers
- favour 'green' environmental policies
- want equality of opportunity, leading to equality of results
- favour high levels of government spending on health, welfare and education
- tend to favour higher levels of taxation on the most wealthy to fund services for the less well-off.

But there are a number of policy areas where the Republicans stand significantly to the right of the UK Conservative Party, over, for example:
- abortion
- death penalty
- same-sex marriage
- renewable energy
- national healthcare
- role of central government in education.

Third and minor parties

REVISED

The different levels of support for third and minor parties in the USA and the UK can be clearly seen by comparing the various elections held in both countries in 2009–10 (see Figure 7.3).

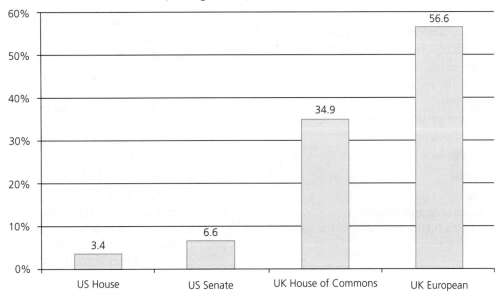

Figure 7.3 Support for third/minor parties in US and UK elections, 2009–10

There are five principal reasons why third parties are so much stronger in the UK than they are in the USA:

- the culture and history of England (UKIP), Scotland (SNP), Wales (Plaid Cymru) and Northern Ireland (unionist parties, SDLP, Sinn Féin)
- Britain's status in Europe (the UKIP issue), with both the major parties taking a pro-EU stance
- third parties in the USA face significant legal and structural barriers – especially regarding ballot access
- the flexible structures of the US parties make them more responsive than their UK counterparts
- the expense of US elections – especially national elections – makes them prohibitive for third parties.

Now test yourself

TESTED ☐

31 Why did legal changes regarding party funding come about in both the USA and the UK?
32 Give three arguments for and three arguments against state funding of political parties.
33 What changes occurred within UK politics that led the UK to move from a two-party to a multiparty system?
34 Give three reasons why factions appear within political parties.
35 Identify three policy areas in which the Republicans in the USA and the Conservatives in the UK basically agree.
36 Identify three policy areas in which the Democrats in the USA and the Labour Party in the UK basically agree.
37 Identify three policy areas in which the Republicans in the USA stand significantly to the right of the Conservatives in the UK.
38 Give three reasons why third parties are much stronger in the UK than in the USA.

Answers on pp. 119–20

The theory of pressure groups

Pressure groups are regarded as having important implications for a modern democracy.

- The theoretical basis of their activity is found in what political theorists call **pluralism** – that political power is distributed among groups representing different interests.
- This stands opposite to the theory of **elitism** – that political power rests with a small, elite group.
- In the pluralist theory of competing groups, the emphasis is on compromise – between competing groups.

Now test yourself

TESTED ☐

39 Define a pressure group.
40 Distinguish between pluralism and elitism.
41 Which of these two theories forms the basis of the existence of pressure groups?

Answers on p. 120

Pressure group: An organised interest group in which members hold similar beliefs and actively pursue ways to influence government.

Pluralism: A theory that political power does not rest simply with the electorate or the governing elite, but is distributed among groups representing widely different interests.

Elitism: A theory that political power rests with a small group who gain power through wealth, family status or intellectual superiority.

Types of pressure groups

Pressure groups are quite different from political parties.

- Political parties seek to win control of government; pressure groups seek to influence those who have control of government.
- They vary considerably in size, wealth and influence.
- They operate at all levels of government – federal, state and local.
- They seek to influence all three branches of the federal and state governments – the legislature, the executive and the judiciary.
- There are numerous typologies of pressure groups (so you can use others and not just the one given below).
- But one easy typology is to divide pressure groups into sectional groups and causal groups.

> **Typical mistake**
>
> Do be careful, therefore, not to give the Green Party as an example of a pressure group. Greenpeace is a pressure group. The Green Party is, of course, a political party.

Sectional groups

REVISED

These groups seek to represent their own section or group within society (see Table 7.1).

Table 7.1 Sectional groups

Type of sectional groups	Examples
Business/trade groups	American Business Conference
	National Association of Manufacturers
	National Automobile Dealers Association
	US Chamber of Commerce
Labour unions	United Auto Workers
	Teamsters (truck drivers)
	American Federation of Labor-Congress of Industrial Organizations (AFL-CIO)
Agricultural groups	American Farm Bureau Federation
	National Farmers Union
	Associated Milk Producers Incorporated
Societal groups	National Organization for Women (NOW)
	National Association for the Advancement of Colored People (NAACP)
	American Association of Retired Persons (AARP)
Professional groups	American Medical Association (AMA)
	National Education Association (NEA)
	American Bar Association (ABA) (lawyers)
Intergovernmental groups	National Governors' Conference
	National Conference of State Legislatures

Causal groups

REVISED

These groups campaign for a particular cause or issue (see Table 7.2).

Table 7.2 Causal groups

Type of causal groups	Examples
Single-interest groups	National Rifle Association (NRA)
	Mothers Against Drunk Driving (MADD)
	National Abortion and Reproductive Rights League (NARAL)
	National Right to Life (NRL)
Ideological groups	American Conservative Union
	People for the American Way
	American Civil Liberties Union (ACLU)
Policy groups	Common Cause
	Friends of the Earth
	The Sierra Club
Think-tanks	Institute for Policy Studies
	Brookings Institution
	Heritage Foundation
	American Enterprise Institute

Now test yourself

TESTED

42 What are sectional groups?
43 Identify three different types of sectional pressure groups and give an example of each.
44 What are causal groups?
45 Identify three different types of causal pressure groups and give an example of each.

Answers on p. 120

Functions of pressure groups

Pressure groups can be said to perform five basic functions, although not all groups perform every function (see Table 7.3).

Table 7.3 Functions of pressure groups

1 Representation	<ul><li>An important link between the public and politicians</li><li>For many Americans this will be the most effective channel of representation for their firmly held views and grievances</li><li>More effective than going directly to their elected officials</li></ul>
2 Citizen participation	• Allows citizens to participate in decision-making between elections
3 Public education	<ul><li>Groups educate and inform public opinion</li><li>Warn of possible dangers</li></ul>
4 Agenda building	<ul><li>Attempt to influence legislators' agenda priorities</li><li>May seek to bring together different groups to achieve a common interest</li></ul>
5 Programme monitoring	• Scrutinise and hold government to account in the implementation of policy

Methods used by pressure groups

Pressure groups use several methods in fulfilling their functions. These include those shown in Table 7.4.

Table 7.4 **How pressure groups fulfil their functions**

1 Electioneering and endorsement	• 1970s' reforms limited the amount any pressure group could give to a candidate in a federal election • This led to setting up of PACs and Super PACs (see Chapter 6) • Groups actively support or oppose presidential or congressional candidates on the basis of candidates' policy positions
2 Lobbying	• Provide vital information to busy legislators and bureaucrats • Hence many groups maintain offices in Washington – 'the K Street corridor' • Many employ former White House staffers and those who have worked in Congress (either as members or as staff) • Groups produce voting cues for members of Congress • They also produce scorecards in which they rate members of Congress on key votes relating to their policy area
3 Organising grassroots activities	• Social media or phone blitzes on Congress • Marches, demonstrations – often aimed at state and federal courthouses and legislatures

Power of pressure groups

> **Exam tip**
>
> It is easy in writing an answer to give the impression that just because a pressure group exists and does something, it is therefore effective and successful. Try to be more subtle in your analysis. State what a group is aiming to achieve, then you can judge whether it is effective or successful.

Pressure groups have had a significant impact in a number of policy areas, including:

1   Environmental protection – groups such as the Sierra Club and the Wilderness Society have pushed for stricter laws for environmental protection and have been at the forefront of opposition to the Trump administration's policy of scaling back on environmental protection.
2   Women's rights – such groups as the League of Women Voters and the National Organization for Women pushed unsuccessfully for passage of the Equal Rights Amendment to the Constitution in the 1970s and 1980s; they are now campaigning on issues such as equal pay and sexual harassment in the workplace.
3   Abortion rights – both pro-life and pro-choice lobbies have been active for the past 40–50 years; they try to be influential not only in the abortion debate but in nomination and confirmation of judicial appointments, especially to the Supreme Court.
4   Gun control – the National Rifle Association is one of the most powerful groups. It seeks to protect Second Amendment rights and opposes tougher gun control legislation. It has found itself more on the defensive following the deaths of 17 people in a Florida high school shooting in February 2018.

> **Typical mistake**
>
> Beware of mixing up 'pro-choice' and 'pro-life'. Pro-choice groups favour a woman's right to *choose* whether to have an abortion; pro-life groups support the right to *life* of the unborn child and are therefore against abortion.

Answers on p. 120

Now test yourself

TESTED

46 Identify three functions of pressure groups.
47 Identify three methods used by pressure groups.
48 Name three policy areas in which pressure groups have been especially influential.

Answers on p. 120

Exam tip

Ensure that you have a wide range of examples of pressure groups – not just the NRA.

Impact of pressure groups on government

Impact on Congress

REVISED

Pressure groups make an impact by:
● directly lobbying members of Congress; attempting to influence legislation and the way members cast their votes
● lobbying congressional committees, especially those who chair or are ranking minority members on relevant committees (see Chapter 2)
● organising constituents – through phone, the internet and social media
● publicising members' voting records and endorsing or opposing candidates.

Impact on the executive

REVISED

They seek to:
● maintain strong ties with relevant executive departments, agencies and bureaus
● influence the drawing up of and enactment of policy within their area of interest.

Impact on the judiciary

REVISED

Pressure groups:
● take a lively interest in nomination and confirmation of judges to the federal courts, especially those to the Supreme Court
● try to influence court hearings through *amicus curiae* (friend of the court) briefings, thereby presenting their views to the court in writing before oral arguments are heard

The American Bar Association (ABA) evaluates the professional qualifications of federal court nominees.

One of the most influential groups is the American Civil Liberties Union (ACLU), which has helped bring high-profile cases to the courts over such issues as protecting affirmative action and, more recently, transgender rights.

Debate

Do we need pressure groups?

Yes, because they...	No, because of...
<ul><li>provide legislators and bureaucrats with useful information and act as a sounding board in policy formulation</li><li>bring some order to the policy debate</li><li>broaden the opportunities for participation in democracy</li><li>can increase levels of accountability for both Congress and the executive</li><li>increase opportunities for representation between elections</li><li>enhance freedom of speech and freedom of association</li></ul>	<ul><li>the **revolving-door syndrome**, which allows former members of Congress or of the executive unfair influence to lobby the institution of which they were once a member</li><li>the **iron-triangle syndrome**, which perpetuates a cosy relationship between pressure groups, the relevant congressional committee(s) and the relevant department or agency</li><li>the inequality of groups – in terms of access, money, size</li><li>their tendency to favour the special interest over the public interest</li><li>allegations of 'buying influence'</li><li>use of direct action that breaks the law, including violence</li></ul>

Revolving-door syndrome: The practice by which former members of Congress (or the executive) take up well-paid jobs with Washington-based lobbying firms, using their expertise and contacts to lobby their previous institution.

Iron-triangle syndrome: A strong relationship between pressure groups, the relevant congressional committees and the relevant government department which attempts to achieve mutually beneficial policy outcomes.

Now test yourself

TESTED

49 Identify two ways in which pressure groups try to impact Congress.
50 Identify ways in which pressure groups try to impact the executive branch.
51 Identify two ways in which pressure groups try to impact the judiciary.
52 Define the term 'revolving-door syndrome'.
53 Define the term 'iron-triangle syndrome'.

Answers on p. 120

Comparing US and UK pressure groups

Electioneering and endorsing

REVISED

There are far more elective posts in the USA than in the UK.
- Presidential, Senate (second chamber) and state elections are all unknown in the UK.
- Plus there is the possibility of primaries in the USA.

- All this means that for structural reasons, US pressure groups have far more opportunities for influence than do their UK counterparts.
- But in the UK, there is an historically close link between organised labour and one of the two major parties (Labour).
- It is true that trade union membership has fallen in recent decades, but the TUC is much more electorally influential in elections in the UK than is the AFL-CIO in the USA.

Lobbying

In terms of lobbying, because of important structural differences, there are far more opportunities for pressure group activity in the USA than in the UK, in all three branches.

Legislature

- The UK Parliament is more controlled and party disciplined than the US Congress.
- The UK Parliament is largely controlled by the executive.
- Therefore, with parties holding more sway at Westminster, pressure groups tend to enjoy less influence.
- But the House of Lords still offers pressure groups opportunities as peers are not subject to party whipping to the same extent as their Commons counterparts.

Executive

- Policy-specific pressure groups will focus on appropriate executive departments – especially in the UK where the legislature provides fewer opportunities for pressure groups.
- In the USA, pressure groups tend to focus more on congressional committees and rather less on executive departments and agencies.
- Again, the difference is largely caused by the structural differences of separation of powers.

Judiciary

- There are significant differences in the political importance of the respective judiciaries.
- Hence lobbying of the courts is much more established in the USA than in the UK because the US courts have the power to interpret a written constitution and can declare laws and actions to be unconstitutional, thereby null and void (see Chapter 4).
- US pressure groups have a long and distinguished history of lobbying the Supreme Court and of being a major player in some landmark decisions concerning, for example:
  ○ equal rights for racial minorities
  ○ abortion
  ○ religious freedoms
  ○ freedom of speech.
- But in the UK, where even the new Supreme Court must operate within a constitutional structure dominated by parliamentary supremacy, and which lacks a codified constitution with entrenched rights, there is no tradition of lobbying the courts.

Grassroots activity

REVISED

Groups in both the USA and the UK organise grassroots activity:

- In the UK, where parties are more centralised and disciplined, this often means trying to influence one of the two major parties.
- In the USA, where parties are less highly centralised, influence is more likely to be aimed at the branches of the federal and state governments.
- In both countries, pressure groups will seek influence through both mass and social media.

What determines success?

REVISED

In both systems, pressure group success will be determined largely by factors such as:

- size of membership
- amount of money available
- the group's strategic position in the political system
- the balance of public opinion
- strength or weakness of countervailing group(s)
- attitude of the administration (USA)/government (UK)
- ability to access the media.

Now test yourself

TESTED

54 Why are there more opportunities for pressure groups to influence elections in the USA than in the UK?

55 Why are there more opportunities for pressure groups to influence the legislature in the USA than in the UK?

56 Why will pressure groups in the UK focus more on the executive branch than on the legislature?

57 Why are there more opportunities for pressure groups to influence the judiciary in the USA than in the UK?

58 Identify four factors that help determine pressure group success.

Answers on p. 120

Summary

You should now have an understanding of:
- party organisation
- party ideology
- party policies
- coalitions of supporters
- the polarisation of American politics
- the two-party system
- third parties
- current conflicts within the parties
- the similarities and differences between political parties in the USA and the UK

- theory of pressure groups
- types of pressure groups
- functions of pressure groups
- methods used by pressure groups
- power of pressure groups
- impact of pressure groups
- arguments for and against pressure groups
- the similarities and differences between pressure groups in the USA and the UK

Exam practice

Section A (comparative)

1 Examine the ways in which the importance of third parties in the USA and the UK differs. [12]
2 Examine the factors that enhance the power of pressure groups in elections in both the
  USA and the UK. [12]

Section B (comparative)

In your answer you must consider the relevance of at least one comparative theory.
1 Analyse the differences in party systems in the USA and the UK. [12]
2 Analyse the differences in the opportunities for pressure groups to influence the judiciary
  in the USA and the UK. [12]

Section C (USA)

In your answer you must consider the stated view and the alternative to this view in a balanced way.
1 Evaluate the extent to which third parties in the USA always lose. [30]
2 Evaluate the extent to which pressure groups are a necessary evil in the US political system. [30]

Answers and quick quiz online

ONLINE

Now test yourself answers

Chapter 1

1 There was virtually no central government at all.
2 A federal form of government; two houses of Congress – one with equal representation for all the states, the other with representation proportional to each state's population; an indirectly elected president.
3 Codified; a blend of vagueness and specificity; entrenched provisions.
4 A constitution that consists of a full and authoritative set of rules written down in a single document.
5 The legislature, the executive and the judiciary.
6 One of: the 'common defence and general welfare clause'; the 'necessary and proper clause'.
7 Enumerated powers are specifically granted by the Constitution; implied powers are merely inferred by the constitution.
8 Reserved powers are those reserved to the states and to the people; concurrent powers are granted to both the federal and state governments.
9 Powers safeguarded by making them difficult to amend or abolish.
10 Either by two-thirds majorities in both houses of Congress, or by the legislatures in two-thirds of the states calling for a national constitutional convention.
11 Either by three-quarters of the state legislatures, or by ratifying conventions in three-quarters of the states.
12 Advantages – three of:
   ○ super-majorities ensure against a small majority being able to impose its will on the majority
   ○ the lengthy and complicated process makes it less likely that the Constitution will be amended on a merely temporary issue
   ○ it ensures that both the federal and state governments must favour a proposal
   ○ it gives a magnified voice to the smaller-population states (through Senate's role and the requirement for agreement of three-quarters of state legislatures)
   ○ provision for a constitutional convention called by the states ensures against a veto being operated by Congress on the initiation of amendments.

Disadvantages – three of:
   ○ it makes it overly difficult for the Constitution to be amended, thereby perpetuating what some see as outdated provisions – for example, the Electoral College
   ○ it makes possible the thwarting of the will of the majority by a small and possibly unrepresentative minority
   ○ the lengthy and complicated process nonetheless allowed the Prohibition amendment to be passed (1918)
   ○ the difficulty of formal amendment enhances power of the (unelected) Supreme Court to make interpretative amendments
   ○ the voice of small-population states is overly represented.
13 The Bill of Rights.
14 Two of:
   ○ slavery prohibited (Thirteenth Amendment, 1865)
   ○ federal government granted power to impose income tax (Sixteenth Amendment, 1913)
   ○ direct election of the Senate (Seventeenth Amendment, 1913)
   ○ two-term limit for the president (Twenty-second Amendment, 1951)
   ○ presidential succession and disability procedures (Twenty-fifth Amendment, 1967)
   ○ voting age lowered to 18 (Twenty-sixth Amendment, 1971).
15 Two of:
   ○ the Founding Fathers created a deliberately difficult process
   ○ the Constitution is, in parts, deliberately vague and has therefore evolved without the need for formal amendment
   ○ the Supreme Court has the power of judicial review (see Chapter 4)
   ○ Americans have become cautious about tampering with the Constitution.
16 Separation of powers, checks and balances, federalism.
17 A theory of government whereby political power is distributed among the legislature, the executive and the judiciary, each acting both independently and interdependently.
18 institutions; powers.

19

President on Congress	Veto a bill
President on federal courts	Nominate judges Pardon
Congress on the president	Amend/delay/reject legislative proposals Override veto Impeachment/trial Refuse to ratify treaties (Senate) Refuse to confirm appointments (Senate)
Congress on federal courts	Propose constitutional amendments Refuse to confirm appointments (Senate)
Federal courts on Congress	Declare law unconstitutional
Federal courts on president	Declare actions unconstitutional

20 A theory of government by which political power is divided between a national government and state governments, each having their own areas of substantive jurisdiction.

21 By:
- the enumerated powers of the federal government
- the implied powers of the federal government
- the concurrent powers of the federal and state governments
- the Tenth Amendment.

22 (a) Any two of: education, Medicaid, Homeland Security and defence, economy and jobs. (b) Any two of: economic stimulus package, expansion of S-CHIP, Medicaid, Obamacare.

23 Any three of:
- variation in state laws on such matters as age at which people can marry, drive a car, or have to attend school; the death penalty
- federal and state courts
- states can act as policy laboratories, experimenting with new solutions to old problems
- all elections are state based and run under state law
- political parties in America are essentially decentralised, state-based parties
- huge federal grants going to the states, as well as the complexity of the tax system because, for example, income tax is levied by both federal and some state governments

- the regions of the South, the Midwest, the Northeast and the West have distinct cultures as well as racial, religious and ideological differences.

24 Any three of:
- liberty
- individualism
- equality
- representative government
- limited government
- states' rights
- gun ownership
- a fear of state-organised religion.

25 Any three of:
- an autocratic monarchy
- the hereditary principle
- the power of a landed aristocracy
- an established church
- a deferential working class
- a lack of social mobility.

26 Any three of:
- primary elections
- congressional committees
- the president's cabinet
- the Executive Office of the President
- the Supreme Court's power of judicial review.

27 Acts of Parliament, common law, the works of Erskine May and Walter Bagehot.

28 Any three of:
- The powers, requirements and rights in the US Constitution are entrenched whereas those in the UK Constitution are not.
- The US Constitution allows for much more popular and democratic participation than does the UK Constitution.
- The US Constitution establishes a separation of powers whereas the UK Constitution establishes more in the way of fused powers, especially between the executive and the legislature.
- Checks and balances are more significant in the US Constitution than in the UK Constitution.
- The US Constitution enshrines the principle of federalism whereas the UK Constitution enshrines the principle of devolution.

Chapter 2

1 Two.
2 House: 435; Senate: 100.
3 House: proportional to state population; Senate: two per state.
4 Women: 83 in House; 21 in Senate. African-Americans: 46 in House; 3 in Senate. Hispanic/Latino: 34 in House; 4 in Senate. Asian: 12 in House; 3 in Senate.

5 ○ Between 1993 and the end of 2018, the House had been controlled by the Democrats for 14 years and the Republicans for 12 years.
○ During the same period, the Senate had been controlled by the Republicans for just over 14 years and by the Democrats for just over 11 years.
○ Only two of Congress's 535 members belong to neither party – senators Bernie Sanders (Vermont) and Angus King (Maine) – but both almost always vote with the Democrats.

6 Law making; oversight; confirmation of appointments.

7 A formal accusation of a serving federal official by a simple majority vote of the House of Representatives.

8 (a) simple majority; (b) two-thirds majority; (c) two-thirds majority.

9 Confirmation of appointments; ratification of treaties.

10 Any three of:
○ senators represent the entire state
○ senators serve longer terms
○ senators are one of only 100
○ senators are more likely to chair a committee or sub-committee
○ the Senate is seen as a recruiting pool for the presidency and vice presidency.

11 Any three of:
○ in passing legislation
○ in conducting oversight of the executive
○ in initiating constitutional amendments
○ in fulfilling a representative function
○ in receiving equal salaries.

12 Any two of: Ted Cruz, Rand Paul, Marco Rubio, Rick Santorum, Lindsey Graham, Hillary Clinton, Bernie Sanders, Jim Webb.

13 Walter Mondale, Dan Quayle, Al Gore, Joe Biden, Mike Pence.

14 Standing committees, select committees, conference committees.

15 18 in the Senate, 30–40 in the House.

16 It reflects the party balance of each respective chamber.

17 They conduct the committee stage of bills; conduct investigations; begin confirmation process of appointments (Senate only).

18 Jim Mattis (26–1); Rex Tillerson (11–10); Steve Mnuchin (11–0); Jeff Sessions (11–9).

19 It prioritises bills coming from the committee stage on to the floor of the House for their debate and votes by giving a 'rule' to a bill setting out the rules of debate, stating whether or not further amendments are permitted.

20 To reconcile the differences between the House and Senate versions of a bill.

21 When an investigation does not fall within the policy area of one standing committee, or when the investigation is likely to be particularly time-consuming.

22 The committee stage is as far as most bills get; committees have full power of amendment; committees have life-and-death power over bills.

23 A device by which one or more senators can delay action on a bill or any other matter by debating it at length or through other obstructive actions.

24 Sign the bill; leave the bill on his desk; veto the bill.

25 (a) The president's power under Article II of the Constitution to return a bill to Congress unsigned, along with the reasons for his objection. (b) A veto power exercised by the president at the end of a legislative session whereby bills not signed are lost.

26 Pass the bill again with a two-thirds majority in both houses.

27 Congressional review and investigation of the activities of the executive branch of government.

28 Any two of:
○ standing committee hearings
○ the subpoena of documents and testimony
○ the Senate's power to confirm appointments
○ the Senate's power to ratify treaties.

29 Because there are no executive branch members present in the legislature.

30 How legislators represent the views of their constituents; how representative legislators are of society as a whole in such matters as race and gender.

31 Trustee model: the legislator makes decisions on behalf of their constituents – the legislator acts as a 'trustee'. Delegate model: the legislator decides in accordance with the views of a majority of their constituents.

32 Any four of:
○ holding party and town hall meetings
○ conducting 'surgeries' with individual constituents
○ making visits around the state/district
○ appearing on local radio phone-ins
○ taking part in interviews with local media
○ addressing various groups in their state/district, e.g. chambers of commerce, Rotary
○ using e-mail and social media.

33 Any three of: political party; the administration; pressure groups; colleagues and staff; personal beliefs.

34 Any three of: the president, the vice president, senior members of the White House staff, the president's congressional liaison staff, cabinet members.

35 Almost all members are either Democrats or Republicans; the two major parties control all leadership positions.

36 Any two of:
- era of 'hyper-partisanship' (Brownstein)
- greater unity within the parties, especially in the House (see Figure 2.1)
- more distinct conflicts between the parties
- big-ticket items tend to pass on strictly party-line votes (e.g. President Trump's tax cuts in December 2017 received no Democrat votes in either house)
- few 'centrists' left in Congress.

37 (a) Partisanship: a situation where members of one party regularly group together to oppose members of another party, characterised by strong party discipline and little cooperation between the parties. (b) Gridlock: failure to get action on policy proposals and legislation in Congress. Gridlock is thought to be exacerbated by divided government and partisanship.

38 Numbers have declined.

39 Party unity has increased significantly in the House over the past decade.

40 Any two of:
- presence/absence of the executive
- chief executive's relationship with the legislature
- rules regarding removal
- party ties/discipline.

41 Similarities, any four of: both bicameral; different parties may control each house; chief executive may not control both houses; both houses have a role in legislation and oversight; committees are important; much oversight conducted by committees; all elections are first-past-the-post. Differences, any four of, that in Congress: both houses are elected; both houses are equal; only two parties represented; executive branch excluded; two- and six-year terms of office; Senate only 100 members; Senate has significant oversight powers; each American has three representatives in Congress.

42 Congress, any two of: federalism; state-based representation; direct election. Parliament, any two of: unitary/devolved structure of the UK; MPs represent parts of historic counties, cities or towns; hereditary principle – landed gentry, established church.

43 The differences concern (any four of): existence or not of a government programme; levels of party discipline; numbers of bills introduced – both total and by individual members; proportion of bills that become law; role of committee stage; nature of standing committees; whether bills are considered by the two chambers concurrently or consecutively; equality of the two chambers in passing legislation; existence of veto power.

44 Congress: standing committee hearings; select committee hearings; confirmation of appointments (Senate); ratification of treaties (Senate); impeachment, trial and removal from office. Parliament: Question Time; selection committee hearings; liaison committee hearings; correspondence with ministers; early day motions; policy debates; Ombudsman; votes of no confidence.

45 Any four of: length of terms of office; number of parties; presence/absence of executive; relative powers compared with upper house; constituencies represented; legislative process; nature and role of standing committees; role of Speaker; onward movement of members to upper house.

46 Any four of: election/hereditary, appointed; number of members; terms of office; role of two major parties; legislative power; oversight powers; onward movement of members.

Chapter 3

1 He can propose, sign and veto legislation.
2 The State of the Union Address.
3 He appoints department and agency heads (e.g. Mike Pompeo); he appoints federal judges, including Supreme Court justices (e.g. Neil Gorsuch).
4 Acts as commander-in-chief of the armed forces; negotiates treaties.
5 On the same ticket as the president.
6 The president can appoint a replacement.
7 Voting in the case of a tied vote in the Senate; becoming president on the death, resignation or removal of the president.
8 The advisory group selected by the president to aid him in making decisions and coordinating the work of the federal government.
9 Because they cannot be both in the cabinet and in Congress.
10 State governors, city mayors, academics, policy specialists.
11 In terms of gender, race, age, region, ideology.
12 Engender team spirit; promote collegiality; exchange information; debate/promote policy, especially 'big-ticket' items.
13 Get to know colleagues; resolve interdepartmental disputes; speak to the president.
14 The umbrella term for the top staff agencies in the White House that assist the president in carrying out the major responsibilities of office.

15 12.
16 Acts as liaison between the White House and the vast federal bureaucracy.
17 Any three of:
  ○ the door-keeper of the Oval Office
  ○ decides for the president whom he sees, what he reads, who speaks to him on the phone
  ○ should act as someone whom sometimes takes the blame for the president if things go wrong
  ○ potentially the most powerful person in the White House after the president.
18 Any two of:
  ○ to advise the president on the allocation of federal funds in the annual budget
  ○ to oversee the spending of all federal departments and agencies
  ○ to act as a clearing house for all legislative and regulatory initiatives coming from the president.
19 To help the president coordinate foreign, security and defence policy.
20 Any three of:
  ○ the State Department
  ○ the Defense Department
  ○ the Central Intelligence Agency (CIA)
  ○ the joint chiefs of staff
  ○ US ambassadors around the world.
21 Any three of:
  ○ While EXOP members work in or near the West Wing, cabinet members work often some geographic distance from the White House.
  ○ While key EXOP members may see the president on a regular basis, some members of the cabinet rarely get to see the president – and certainly not one on one.
  ○ Therefore, while EXOP members often know what the president wants from day to day, cabinet members often feel out of the loop.
  ○ While EXOP members work only for the president, cabinet members have divided loyalties – to the president, but also to Congress, to their bureaucracy and to client pressure groups.
  ○ EXOP staff therefore often regard cabinet members as being disloyal.
22 (a) Amend, delay or reject legislation; (b) override the veto by a two-thirds majority in both houses; (c) Senate must confirm; (d) Senate must ratify.
23 Any three of:
  ○ the vice president
  ○ the Office of Legislative Affairs (part of the White House Office)
  ○ cabinet officers
  ○ party leadership in Congress.
24 Any three of:
  ○ phone calls
  ○ support legislation important to a member of Congress
  ○ invitations – social or political – to the White House
  ○ campaign for them (only for members from the president's party)
  ○ go on TV to appeal directly to voters and ask them to contact their members of Congress and tell them to support him.
25 'Bargainer-in-chief'.
26 An annual statistic that measures how often the president won in recorded votes in Congress on which he took a clear position, expressed as a percentage of all such votes. Obama's score varied widely because the score tends to be higher in the first term and when the president's party controls both houses of Congress.
27 An official document issued by the executive branch with the effect of law, through which the president directs federal officials to take certain actions.
28 Because they are easy for a president to issue.
29 A statement issued by the president on signing a bill, which may challenge specific provisions of the bill on constitutional or other grounds.
30 Critics claim they are an abuse of presidential power over legislation; supporters see them as a way of the president getting his way over legislation even when Congress is uncooperative.
31 A temporary appointment of a federal official made by the president to fill a vacancy while the Senate is in recess.
32 Another way of the president getting his way against an uncooperative Congress – this time gridlock in the Senate over confirmation of appointments.
33 A presidency characterised by the misuse of presidential powers, particularly excessive secrecy – especially in foreign policy – and high-handedness in dealing with Congress. Associated with Richard Nixon.
34 A presidency characterised by ineffectiveness and weakness, resulting from congressional overassertiveness. Associated with Gerald Ford and Jimmy Carter.
35 Characterised by presidential reassertiveness but power that is often limited by a new era of hyper-partisanship.
36 To act as commander-in-chief of the armed forces; to negotiate treaties with foreign powers; to make certain appointments, e.g. Secretary of State, Secretary of Defense, Director of the CIA, ambassadors.

37 Any three of:
- ○ to declare war (but not used since 1941)
- ○ control of the budget (including military spending)
- ○ to ratify treaties (Senate only)
- ○ to confirm appointments (Senate only)
- ○ to investigate (through such committees as the Senate Foreign Relations Committee, the House Armed Services Committee).

38 Any three of:
- ○ amend, delay, reject the president's legislative proposals and budgetary requests
- ○ override the president's veto
- ○ refuse to ratify treaties (Senate)
- ○ refuse to confirm appointments (Senate)
- ○ investigate the president's actions and policies
- ○ impeach, try and remove the president from office.

39 May declare the president's actions to be unconstitutional.

40 Any three of: public opinion; pressure groups; voters; federal bureaucracy; state governments.

41 Any three of: electoral mandate; public approval; first/second term; unified/divided government; crises.

42 People tend to 'rally round the flag' and look to the president for leadership.

43 Any four of:
- ○ the presidency is the product of revolution; the PM is the product of evolution
- ○ the president is elected by the people; the PM is elected as party leader by the party
- ○ the president is entirely separate from the legislature; the PM is a member of the legislature
- ○ the president is limited to two terms; there are no term limits for the PM
- ○ the president is aided by an advisory cabinet; the PM has a cabinet that is more than merely advisory
- ○ the president can be removed only by impeachment; the PM may be removed as leader by their party, or as a consequence of losing a confidence vote in the House of Commons.

44 Any four of:
- ○ the president fulfils roles of head of state and chief executive; the PM is only chief executive
- ○ the president has formal input only at the start and finish of the legislative process; the PM draws up the government's legislative programme
- ○ the president appoints cabinet subject to Senate confirmation; the PM appoints cabinet without formal checks

- ○ the president acts as commander-in-chief but only Congress can declare war; the PM can use the royal prerogative to declare war and deploy troops abroad
- ○ the president has an elected VP, who automatically succeeds if the president dies, resigns or is removed from office; the PM may appoint an unofficial deputy PM
- ○ the president has a large EXOP; the PM has a small Number 10 staff plus Cabinet Office
- ○ the president submits annual budget to Congress, which forms the basis for negotiations with Congress; the PM submits annual budget to Parliament, which is usually passed without significant amendment
- ○ the president appoints all federal judges; the PM has no such power
- ○ the president has a pardon power; the PM has no such power.

45 The doctrine of the separation of powers – that the president is entirely separate from Congress.

46 Because of the significant differences in powers, role, membership, meetings, relationship with president/PM.

Chapter 4

1 Nine.

2 The president.

3 By the Senate, simple majority required.

4 For life, or until they voluntarily retire.

5 Voluntary resignation, removal through impeachment, or death.

6 Strict constructionist: a Supreme Court justice who interprets the Constitution strictly or literally and tends to stress the retention of power by individual states. Loose constructionist: a Supreme Court justice who interprets the Constitution less literally and tends to stress the broad grants of power to the federal government.

7 Strict: Roberts, Thomas, Alito, Gorsuch. Loose: Ginsburg, Breyer, Sotomayor, Kagan.

8 Swing justice.

9 A Supreme Court justice who interprets the Constitution in line with the meaning or intent of the framers at the time of enactment.

10 They would consider the Constitution as a dynamic, living document, interpretation of which should take account of the views of contemporary society.

11 The five-stage process is:
- ○ A vacancy occurs.
- ○ The president instigates a search for possible nominees and interviews short-listed candidates.
- ○ The president announces his nominee.

- The Senate Judiciary Committee holds a confirmation hearing on the nomineė and makes a recommendatory vote.
- The nomination is debated and voted on in the full Senate. A simple majority vote is required for confirmation.

12 Voting is now usually along party lines.

13 Any three of:
- Presidents have tended to politicise the nominations by attempting to choose justices who share their political views and judicial philosophy (e.g. Obama with Kagan; Trump with Gorsuch).
- The Senate has tended to politicise the confirmation process by focusing more on hot-button issues (e.g. women's rights) than on qualifications.
- Members of the Senate Judiciary Committee from the president's party tend to ask soft questions of the nominee.
- Members of the Senate Judiciary Committee from the opposition party attempt, through their questions, to attack or embarrass the nominee rather than to elicit relevant information.
- Justices are now frequently confirmed on party-line votes (e.g. Gorsuch).
- The media conduct a 'feeding frenzy' often connected with matters of trivia.

14 Any three of:
- they occur infrequently
- they are for life
- just one new appointee to a nine-member body can significantly change its philosophical balance
- the Supreme Court has the power of judicial review
- their decisions will profoundly affect the lives of ordinary Americans for generations to come.

15 The power of the Supreme Court to declare Acts of Congress, actions of the executive, or Acts or actions of state governments unconstitutional.

16 It was 'found' by the Court in *Marbury v Madison* (1803) – regarding a federal law – and used again in *Fletcher v Peck* (1810) – regarding a state law.

17 Because the effects of its decisions have almost the effect of a law having been passed by Congress.

18 An approach to judicial decision making that holds that judges should use their position to promote desirable social ends, even if that means overturning the decisions of elected officials.

19 Any two of:
- *Roe v Wade* (1973) – guaranteed a woman's right to choose an abortion.
- *District of Columbia v Heller* (2008) – guaranteed individual gun ownership rights.

- *Obergefell v Hodges* (2015) – guaranteed rights to same-sex marriage.

20 An approach to judicial decision making that holds that judges should defer to the legislative and executive branches, and to precedent established in previous Court decisions.

21 A legal principle that judges should look to past precedents as a guide wherever possible (literally, 'let the decision stand').

22 Any two of:
- *Zelman v Simmons-Harris* (2002): the Court upheld an Ohio state programme giving financial aid to parents, allowing them, if they so chose, to send their children to a religious or private school.
  Significance: state government money could be finding its way to a religious, private school.
- *Town of Greece v Galloway* (2014): the Court allowed legislative bodies (such as town councils) to begin their meetings with prayer.
  Significance: strengthened individual rights to practise their religion in public, even in state-constituted and state-funded bodies.
- *Burwell v Hobby Lobby Stores Inc* (2010): the Court overturned the requirement under the Affordable Care Act (2010) (otherwise known as Obamacare) that family-owned firms had to pay for health insurance coverage for contraception as this violated the religious beliefs of some Christian-run companies.
  Significance: strengthened individual rights of Christian business executives to run their companies along lines that agreed with their religious beliefs.

23 Any two of:
- *McConnell v Federal Election Commission* (2004): upheld federal law (Bipartisan Campaign Reform Act) banning soft money in election campaigns, stating that this ban did not violate freedom of speech.
  Significance: limiting campaign finance is not incompatible with the freedom of speech provision of the Constitution.
- *Citizens United v FEC* (2010): ruled that when it comes to rights of political speech, business corporations and labour unions have the same rights as individuals.
  Significance: opened the door to unlimited spending by corporations in election campaigns, mostly funnelled through PACs.
- *McCutcheon v FEC* (2014): the Court struck down a 1970s limit on totals that wealthy individuals can contribute to candidates and PACs.
  Significance: reaffirmed giving of money to candidates and PACs as a fundamental right.

24 Never before had the courts ruled this interpretation of the Second Amendment.

25 The Court was clearly seen as telling us what 18th-century words mean in 21st-century America.

26 Any two of:
- ○ *Roe v Wade* (1973): ruled that the state law of Texas forbidding abortion was unconstitutional.
  Significance: guaranteed a woman's right to choose an abortion as a constitutionally protected right.
- ○ *Gonzales v Carhart* (2007): upheld the Partial Birth Abortion Act (2003), which banned late-term abortions.
  Significance: established that a woman's right to choose an abortion could be legally limited.
- ○ *Whole Woman's Health v Hellerstedt* (2016): struck down as unconstitutional two parts of a Texas state law concerning abortion provision.
  Significance: not all limits on a woman's right to choose would be regarded as constitutionally permissible.

27 Any two of:
- ○ *United States v Windsor* (2013): declared the Defense of Marriage Act (1996) to be unconstitutional and that it is unconstitutional to treat same-sex married couples differently from other married couples in terms of federal benefits.
- ○ *Obergefell v Hodges* (2015): declared that state bans on same-sex marriage were unconstitutional.

28 *National Federation of Independent Business v Sebelius* (2012).

29 *National Labor Relations Board v Noel Canning* (2014).

30 Any two of:
- ○ the Senate has the power to confirm or reject appointments
- ○ Congress fixes the numerical size of the Court
- ○ Congress has the power of impeachment – even the threat of impeachment is a check
- ○ Congress can initiate constitutional amendments that would have the effect of overturning the Court's decision.

31 He has the power to nominate justices; can decide whether or not to throw his political weight behind a decision of the Court, thereby either enhancing or decreasing the Court's perceived legitimacy.

32 Any two of:
- ○ the Court has no power of initiation: it must wait for cases to be brought before it
- ○ the Court has no enforcement powers: it is dependent on the other branches of government and/or the rule of law for implementation of and obedience to Court decisions
- ○ public opinion: if the Court makes decisions that are regarded as wrong by a majority of the public, the Court loses some of its legitimacy
- ○ the Court is checked by itself – by decisions it has already made
- ○ the Court is checked by the Constitution – although certain parts of the Constitution are open to the Court's interpretation, other parts are very specific.

33 US Supreme Court created by Founding Fathers in 1787; UK Supreme Court created by Act of Parliament in 2009. US Supreme Court written into the Constitution; UK Supreme Court written into Act of Parliament. US Supreme Court was the first federal court to be created; UK Supreme Court was the last UK court to be created.

34 US system based on 'separated institutions, sharing powers' while the UK system based on 'fused powers'. US system was the product of revolution while the UK system is the product of evolution.

35 US: nominated by the president and confirmed by the Senate. UK: nominated by the Judicial Appointments Commission (no confirmation required).

36 US: life tenure. UK: must retire at 70 if appointed after 1995, otherwise must retire at 75.

37 Latin phrase (literally, 'beyond the powers') used to describe an action that is beyond one's legal power or authority. It is important in the UK Supreme Court because it centres on the Court's tendency to declare the actions of ministers *ultra vires*.

38 Any three of: the executive, the legislature, pressure groups, the media, other (senior) judges.

39 Any two of: judges' immunity from prosecution for acts carried out as judges; immunity from lawsuits of defamation for what they say while hearing cases; salaries cannot be reduced.

Chapter 5

1 Civil rights: positive acts of government designed to protect persons against arbitrary or discriminatory treatment by government or individuals. Civil liberties: those liberties, mostly spelt out in the Constitution, that guarantee the protection of persons, expression and property from arbitrary interference by government.

2 Any three of: legislation; constitutional amendment; decision of the Supreme Court; presidential leadership; citizen action.

3 Rights of the physically disabled by the Americans with Disabilities Act (1990); gay rights by *Obergefell v Hodges* (2015).

4 A programme giving members of a previously disadvantaged minority group a head start in, for example, higher education or employment.

5 The mandated movement of school children between racially homogeneous neighbourhoods – white suburbs and black inner cities – to create racially mixed schools.

6 A programme by which a certain percentage (quota) of places in, for example, higher education or employment are reserved for people from previously disadvantaged minorities.

7 Equality of opportunity focuses on giving the same rights and opportunities to all. Equality of results focuses on outcomes – on giving advantages to previously disadvantaged groups.

8 Any two of: *Gratz v Bollinger* (2003); *Grutter v Bollinger* (2003); *Parents Involved v Seattle School District* (2007); *Fisher v University of Texas* (2013 and 2016).

9 Advantages: any three of:
   ○ leads to greater levels of diversity
   ○ rights previous wrongs – those previously disadvantaged are now advantaged
   ○ opens up areas of education and employment that otherwise would be out of the reach of disadvantaged minorities
   ○ in education, creates a more diverse student body, thereby promoting integration and racial tolerance.

   Disadvantages: any three of:
   ○ advantage for one group leads to disadvantage for other groups – 'reverse discrimination'
   ○ can lead to minorities being admitted to higher education courses and jobs with which they are ill equipped to cope
   ○ can be condescending to minorities
   ○ perpetuates a society based on colour and race.

10 Any two of:
   ○ legislation, e.g. Voting Rights Act (1965) and the re-authorisation of key parts of this Act in 2006
   ○ voter registration drives among black and Hispanic communities
   ○ voter turnout drives among the same groups.

11 Either introduction by some states of photo ID requirement at polling stations; or removal of voting rights following criminal convictions.

12 Black members up from 16 in 1979–80 to 49 in 2017–18; Hispanic/Latino members up from 6 in 1979–80 to 38 in 2017–18.

13 Any two of: Ben Carson, Bobby Jindal, Marco Rubio.

14 Out of 15 heads of executive departments, 7 were from ethnic minorities.

15 Got Congress to pass the Development, Relief, and Education for Alien Minors (DREAM) Act. Also created the DACA programme.

16 Deferred Action for Childhood Arrivals (2012), which allowed some individuals who entered the country as the children of illegal immigrants to have the temporary right to live, study and work in the USA.

17 Announced his intention to end the DACA programme, make the deportation of all illegal immigrants a top priority, and build a wall along the USA–Mexico border.

18 In the USA, rights are entrenched in a codified constitution.

19 The Constitution, Acts of Congress, decisions of the Supreme Court.

20 Acts of Parliament, decisions of the courts.

21 Supporters of same-sex marriage and orthodox Christians.

22 Effective protection of rights v. the need for security.

23 In the USA: ACLU and NAACP; in the UK: Liberty and Stonewall.

Chapter 6

1 Every four years.

2 A natural-born American citizen; at least 35 years of age; resident in the USA for at least 14 years.

3 Limits presidents to two full terms in office.

4 The period between candidates declaring an intention to run for the presidency and the first primaries and caucuses.

5 The calendar year before the presidential election.

6 Any three of:
   ○ candidate announcements
   ○ televised party debates
   ○ fundraising
   ○ raising national name recognition for lesser-known candidates
   ○ opinion polls showing who are the front-runners
   ○ endorsements by leading party figures (e.g. members of Congress, state governors, former presidents).

7 A primary is an election; a caucus is a meeting.

8 Show popularity of presidential candidates; choose delegates to go to the national party conventions.

9 (a) A Tuesday in February or early March when a number of states coincide their presidential primaries and caucuses to try to gain influence.

(b) The phenomenon by which states schedules their primaries or caucuses earlier in the nomination cycles in an attempt to increase their importance.

10 Open primary: any registered voter may vote in either primary. Closed primary: only registered Republicans can vote in the Republican primary and only registered Democrats can vote in the Democratic primary.

11 Proportional primary: delegates are awarded to candidates in proportion to the votes they get; winner-take-all primary: winner of the popular vote wins all the delegates.

12 Primaries and caucuses are still held but little attention is given to them.

13 Turnout is low: 20–30% on average in primaries; much lower in caucuses.

14 (a) Reasons why they are important – any three of:
   ○ the presidential candidates emerge during them
   ○ a large number of candidates are eliminated by them
   ○ delegates (who make the final decision about the candidate) are chosen by them
   ○ they attract a large amount of media attention
   ○ lesser-known candidates see them as a way of boosting name recognition
   ○ they test some presidential skills (e.g. oratorical, presentational, organisational)
   ○ they are much more important than they used to be before the McGovern–Fraser reforms (1970s).

(b) Reasons why they are not important – any three of:
   ○ primaries often merely confirm decisions made during the 'invisible primary' (i.e. the candidates leading in the polls at the start of the primaries are the ones eventually chosen)
   ○ what goes on in the media (e.g. televised candidate debates) is often more important
   ○ many presidential skills are not tested (e.g. ability to compromise, ability to work with Congress)
   ○ many primaries choose so few delegates that they cannot be regarded as important.

15 (a) Strengths – any three of:
   ○ increased levels of participation by voters
   ○ increased choice of candidates
   ○ process opened up to outside candidates (e.g. Obama, Trump)
   ○ a gruelling race for a gruelling job.

(b) Weaknesses – any three of:
   ○ can lead to voter apathy
   ○ voters are often unrepresentative
   ○ process is too long, too expensive, too dominated by the media
   ○ can develop into bitter personal battles
   ○ lack of 'peer review'
   ○ role of 'super-delegates' (Democrats).

16 Choosing the presidential candidate; choosing the vice presidential candidate; deciding the party platform.

17 Promoting party unity; enthusing the party faithful; enthusing ordinary voters.

18 (a) Are important – any three of:
   ○ the only time the national parties meet together
   ○ provide an opportunity to promote party unity after the primaries
   ○ provide an opportunity to enthuse the party faithful to go and campaign for the ticket
   ○ introduce the presidential candidates to the public
   ○ delivery of the acceptance speech
   ○ can lead to a significant 'bounce' in the polls
   ○ many voters don't tune in to the campaign until the conventions start
   ○ a significant number of voters make their decision about whom to vote for at this stage.

(b) Are not important – any three of:
   ○ nowadays they make few (if any) significant decisions; merely confirm decisions made earlier that we already know about
   ○ television coverage has become much reduced
   ○ ordinary voters don't really see them as important
   ○ those held when the party is nominating the sitting president for re-election can be pretty devoid of any real significance
   ○ more balloons, hoopla and celebrities than serious policy debate and presentation.

19 Labor Day (first Monday in September).

20 Nine weeks.

21 An event occurring late in the presidential campaign to the disadvantage of one candidate, leaving that candidate with little or no time to recover before Election Day.

22 A political committee that raises limited amounts of money and spends contributions for the express purpose of electing or defeating candidates.

23 Any three of:
   ○ national party committees banned from raising or spending 'soft money'
   ○ labour unions and corporations forbidden from directly funding issue ads

○ unions and corporations forbidden from financing ads that mention a federal candidate within 60 days of a general election or 30 days of a primary

○ increased individual limits on contributions to individual candidates or candidate committees

○ banned contributions from foreign nationals

○ provided for a 'stand by your ad' verbal endorsement by candidates on TV ads.

24 Commission on Presidential Debates.

25 Podiums, town hall, round table.

26 Any three of:
○ can play a decisive role in the campaign (e.g. 1980, 2012)
○ can affect the opinion polls
○ especially important for the challenging candidate who will be less well known
○ a good sound bite from a candidate will be played repeatedly in the media in the days that follow
○ a gaffe can seriously affect a candidate's chances of success (e.g. Gore in 2000).

27 Any three of:
○ in 2016, polls found that Clinton easily won all three debates, yet she lost the election
○ Trump's numerous debate gaffes did not seriously affect his poll numbers
○ policy detail is rarely discussed
○ they are not really 'debates', more the trotting out of rehearsed lines and catch-phrases
○ viewership has tended to decline (though it was up in 2016).

28 Fixed as the Tuesday after the first Monday in November.

29 More than 30.

30 Dropped steadily from 1960 to 1996, then increased in 2000–08, but fell again in 2016.

31 Three: Gerald Ford, Jimmy Carter, George H.W. Bush.

32 Equal to each state's representation in Congress.

33 270.

34 Winner-take-all.

35 Maine and Nebraska: winner in each congressional district wins one electoral vote; the state-wide winner wins the remaining two electoral votes.

36 An Elector in the Electoral College who casts their ballot for a candidate other than the one who won the popular vote in their state. See Table 6.6 for examples.

37 Preserves the voice of the small-population states; usually results in a two-horse race.

38 Any four of:
○ small-population states are over-represented
○ winner-take-all system can distort the result
○ possible for the loser of the popular vote to win the Electoral College vote

○ unfair to national third parties
○ 'rogue' or 'faithless' Electors
○ potential problem if Electoral College is deadlocked.

39 Direct election; congressional district system; proportional system.

40 Any two of:
○ there is no widespread consensus on a better alternative
○ highly unlikely that any significant reform would be legislatively or constitutionally doable
○ the suggested reforms also have significant problems.

41 All of the House; one-third of the Senate.

42 Elections for the whole of the House and one-third of the Senate that occur midway through a president's four-year term.

43 By minimum age (House 25, Senate 30); by length of citizenship (House 7 years, Senate 9 years).

44 A state law that requires House members to be resident in the congressional district they represent.

45 Any two of:
○ their ability to provide federal funding for constituency/state projects
○ high levels of name recognition
○ fundraising advantages: incumbents can usually raise much more than challengers can.

46 The effect when an extremely popular candidate at the top of the ticket (e.g. for president or governor) carries candidates for lower offices with him/her into office.

47 Voting for candidates of the same party for different offices at the same election.

48 Any two of:
○ it makes it much harder for party control of the House to change hands
○ members from safe districts are more likely to cast party line votes than are those from competitive ones
○ it therefore increases levels of partisanship.

49 Without the winning presidential candidate on the ticket, House members from the president's party do less well; voters see the midterms as an opportunity to express disappointment/disapproval with the president.

Chapter 7

1 Federalism.

2 National committee, national chair, national convention.

3 Any three of:
○ new campaign finance laws resulted in money flowing to the national parties and the

candidates themselves rather than being raised by the state or local parties
- television provided a medium through which candidates could appeal directly to voters, thereby cutting out state and local parties that had traditionally been the medium
- emergence of sophisticated opinion polls allowed candidates to directly 'hear' what voters were saying without actually meeting them
- new technology allowed national parties to set up sophisticated fundraising and direct mailing operations – later also via social media
- parties became more ideologically cohesive
- national parties played a larger role in recruitment and training of congressional candidates.

4 The national chairs.

5 State, congressional district, county, city, ward, precinct.

6 A collectively held set of beliefs.

7 Democrats = liberal; Republicans = conservative.

8 Social conservatives focus on issues such as abortion and same-sex marriage; fiscal conservatives focus on issues such as the national debt, federal budget deficit and taxation.

9 Any four of:
- increased spending on social welfare programmes
- death penalty
- gun control
- high levels of defence spending
- stricter environmental controls
- stricter controls on immigration
- 'Obamacare'.

10 The Democratic Party.

11 The Republican Party.

12 Any four of: small town/rural, conservatives, white, men, over 65, 45–64, high school only educated.

13 Any four of: blacks, liberals, Hispanics, Asians, city, 18–29, women, earning less than $30K.

14 The gap between the support given to a candidate by women and the support given to the same candidate by men.

15 The Democrats tend to take policy positions more favoured by women on (any three of):
- abortion rights (support)
- capital punishment (oppose)
- gun control (support)
- lower levels of defence spending (support).

16 Any three of:
- they felt neglected by Washington politicians of both parties who had made promises to them during campaigns but had failed to deliver once elected
- the effects of the 2008–09 economic crash – they believed that whereas the government

bailed out banks and big business, they were left unemployed and unhelped
- they believed that their values, way of life and beliefs (e.g. in traditional marriage) had been swept aside and sneered at by a 'liberal elite'
- they felt that the America in which they grew up – overwhelmingly white and nominally Christian – was fast disappearing.

17 His 'Make America Great Again' theme.

18 Any three of: Ohio, Florida, Virginia, North Carolina.

19 Protestants and those who attend places of worship regularly tend to vote Republican; Catholics and those who attend places of worship rarely tend to vote Democrat.

20 Any five of:
- predominantly white
- overwhelmingly Protestant (and especially evangelical)
- rural, small town or suburban
- fiscally and socially conservative
- pro-guns
- pro-life
- pro-traditional marriage
- support limited role for federal government
- opposed to Obamacare
- watch Fox News.

21 Any five of:
- a racial rainbow of white, black, Asian, Hispanic/Latino
- urban
- socially liberal
- support gun control measures
- pro-choice
- pro-gay rights
- support an expansive role for federal government
- support Obamacare
- watch CNN and *Saturday Night Live*.

22 A party system in which two major parties regularly win the vast majority of the votes, capture nearly all of the seats in the legislature and alternately control the executive.

23 Any three of:
- Popular vote – in all the last seven presidential elections, two major parties have won more than 80% of the popular vote, on four occasions exceeding 95%.
- Congressional seats – after 2016, two major parties controlled 533 of the 535 seats in Congress.
- Executive branch control – every president since 1853 has been a Democrat or a Republican.
- State government – by 2017, 49 of the 50 state governors were either Democrats or Republicans.

24 Electoral system; broad party ideologies; primary elections.

25 National (Libertarian Party, Green Party); regional (American Independence Party in 1968); state (New York Conservative Party).

26 Any two of:
- might be thought to have little or no impact as they rarely win a significant number of votes
- but might be thought to have some significant impact in that they can:
  – influence the outcome even with a very small percentage of the votes (e.g. 2000)
  – influence the policy agenda of the two major parties (e.g. the Green Party)
- third parties can have some impact within certain states.

27 Any three of:
- Electoral system: first-past-the-post, winner-take-all system makes it very difficult for third parties to win.
- Ballot access laws: third parties are disadvantaged by laws regulating how candidates must qualify for the ballot in each of the 50 states.
- Lack of resources: difficulties in raising significant amounts of money result in little to spend on campaigning, advertising, organisation, get-out-the vote operations.
- Lack of media coverage: not newsworthy; cannot afford TV advertising; excluded from TV debates.
- Co-optation of their policies: major parties may co-opt their policies, thereby depriving them of future success.

28 Any three of:
- they lost the presidential election in 2016 – though their candidate won nearly 3 million more votes than her opponent
- from 2008 to 2016 they lost 10 seats in the Senate and 61 in the House, losing control of both chambers
- during the same period the number of Democrat governors fell from 29 to 16
- they lost nearly 1,000 state legislative seats during the same eight-year period
- at state level, the party in 2017 was at its lowest electoral level since 1925.

29 Conflict between the liberal wing and the establishment wing.

30 Tea Party, Freedom Caucus, establishment versus Trump.

31 USA: federal matching funds; UK: Short Money.

32 Arguments for, any three of:
- end parties' dependence on wealthy donors
- enable parties to better perform their democratic functions – organisation, representation, creating policy priorities
- fill the gap created by falling membership
- lead to greater transparency
- help equalise parties' financial resources
- make it easier to limit spending
- encourage greater public engagement if funding were linked to electoral turnout.

Arguments against, any three of:
- reinforce the financial advantage of major parties
- further increase disconnect between parties and voters
- diminish belief in the principle that citizen participation is voluntary
- lead to objections from tax payers whose money would go to parties they don't support
- reinforce the parties' role, which many see as an anachronism in the digital age.

33 The rise of nationalism in Scotland, Wales and Northern Ireland.

34 Any three of:
- to accentuate certain policies
- to focus on a particular ideological aspect
- to reflect geographic, ethnic, economic, generational, religious groups
- to widen voter appeal
- to extol the party 'greats'
- to challenge the party establishment.

35 Any three of:
- dislike big government
- favour low taxation
- strong on law and order
- high levels of defence spending
- focus on equality of opportunity rather than equality of results.

36 Any three of:
- rights of minorities
- rights of workers
- green policies
- equality of results
- high levels of government spending on social welfare and education
- higher levels of tax for the wealthy to fund services for the poor.

37 Any three of:
- abortion
- death penalty
- same-sex marriage
- renewable energy
- national healthcare
- role of central government in education.

38 Any three of:
- the culture and history of England (UKIP), Scotland (SNP), Wales (Plaid Cymru) and Northern Ireland (unionist parties, SDLP, Sinn Féin)
- Britain's status in Europe (the UKIP issue), with both the major parties taking a pro-EU stance
- third parties in the USA face significant legal and structural barriers – especially regarding ballot access
- the flexible structures of the US parties make them more responsive than their UK counterparts
- the expense of US elections – especially national elections – makes them prohibitive for third parties.

39 An organised interest group in which members hold similar beliefs and actively pursue ways to influence government.

40 Pluralism: a theory that political power does not rest simply with the electorate or the governing elite, but is distributed among groups representing widely different interests. Elitism: a theory that political power rests with a small group who gain power through wealth, family status or intellectual superiority.

41 Pluralism.

42 Groups that seek to represent their own section or group within society.

43 Any three of: business/trade; labour; agricultural; societal; professional; intergovernmental. See Table 7.1 for examples.

44 Groups that campaign for a particular cause or issue.

45 Any three of: single-interest; ideological; policy; think-tanks. See Table 7.2 for examples.

46 Any three of: representation; citizen participation; public education; agenda building; programme monitoring.

47 Electioneering/endorsing; lobbying; organising grassroots activities.

48 Any three of: environmental protection, women's rights, abortion, gun control.

49 Any two of:
- by directly lobbying members of Congress; attempting to influence legislation and the way members cast their votes
- by lobbying congressional committees, especially those who chair or are ranking minority members on relevant committees (see Chapter 2)
- by organising constituents – through phone, the internet and social media
- by publicising members' voting records and endorsing or opposing candidates.

50 Seek to maintain strong ties with relevant executive departments, agencies and bureaus; seek to influence the drawing up of and enactment of policy within their area of interest.

51 Any two of:
- take a lively interest in nomination and confirmation of judges to the federal courts, especially those to the Supreme Court
- the American Bar Association (ABA) evaluates the professional qualifications of nominees
- try to influence court hearings through *amicus curiae* (friend of the court) briefings, thereby presenting their views to the court in writing before oral arguments are heard
- one of the most influential groups is the American Civil Liberties Union (ACLU) which has helped bring high-profile cases to the courts over such issues as protecting affirmative action, and more recently on the issue of transgender rights.

52 The practice by which former members of Congress (or the executive) take up well-paid jobs with Washington-based lobbying firms, using their expertise and contacts to lobby their previous institution.

53 A strong relationship between pressure groups, the relevant congressional committees and the relevant government department, which attempts to achieve mutually beneficial policy outcomes.

54 Far more elective posts in the USA.

55 Congressional parties tend to be weaker.

56 More likely to be effective as Parliament is very party dominated.

57 The judiciary in the USA has greater political importance.

58 Any four of:
- size of membership
- amount of money available
- the group's strategic position in the political system
- the balance of public opinion
- strength or weakness of countervailing group(s)
- attitude of the administration (USA)/government (UK)
- ability to access the media.